NORMAL

BY THE SAME AUTHOR

COME TO ME
(*Stories*)

LOVE INVENTS US
(*Novel*)

A BLIND MAN CAN SEE HOW MUCH I LOVE YOU
(*Stories*)

NORMAL

TRANSSEXUAL CEOS,
CROSSDRESSING COPS,
AND HERMAPHRODITES
WITH ATTITUDE

AMY BLOOM

BLOOMSBURY

First published in Great Britain 2003

Portions of this work were originally published, in different form,
in *The Atlantic* and *The New Yorker*

Bloomsbury Publishing Plc, 38 Soho Square, London W1D 3HB

A CIP catalogue record for this book is available from the British Library

ISBN 0 7475 6456 6

10 9 8 7 6 5 4 3 2 1

Printed in Great Britain by Clays Ltd, St Ives plc

www.bloomsbury.com

IN MEMORIAM

MALCOLM KEITH, MY TEACHER

1923–2001

CONTENTS

ACKNOWLEDGMENTS

I have been thinking and talking about gender, sex, sexuality, culture, health, and illness for the last eight years, and I could not have completed this book without the advice, insights, and writings of the following people, whose help was even greater than I have indicated in these pages: Mariette Pathy Allen, Kay Ariel, Ray Blanchard, Cheryl Chase, Ken Corbett, Dallas Denny, Holly Devor, Mickey Diamond, Mark Doty, Alice Domurat Dreger, Peter Edidin, the Fairfaxes, Lori Fox, James Green, Philip Gruppuso, Judith Halberstam, Suzanne Kessler, Don Laub, Arthur Lavin, Gail Lebovic, Steve Levine, Merissa Sherrill Lynn, Donald Moon, Angela Moreno, Esther Newton, Rachel Pollack, Marc Rubinstein, the Rudds, Leah Schaefer, SPICE, and Sydney Spiesel.

A number of people preferred not to be identified; to all of you who helped me gather information, clarify my thoughts, and better understand things that are not so easy to understand, thank you.

To my agent, Phyllis Wender, extraordinary mix of dear friend, fearless watchdog, and Natty Bumppo, and to my editor, Kate Medina, who believed in this project from its inception and guided me through it with her usual rare deft grace and high standards, I am able to convey only a fraction of my appreciation.

I was also helped by the intelligent conversation, suggestions, and observations of my three dearest critics, Alex, Caitlin, and Sarah, and by the unending encouragement and support of my best reader, editor, and beloved, Joy Johannessen.

PREFACE

A great multitude of people are continually talking of the Law of Nature; and then they go on giving you their sentiments about what is right and what is wrong: and these sentiments, you are to understand, are so many chapters and sections of the Law of Nature. . . . [Such and such an act, they say,] is unnatural, that is, repugnant to nature: for I do not like to practise it: and, consequently, do not practise it. It is therefore repugnant to what ought to be the nature of everybody else.

JEREMY BENTHAM,

Introduction to the Principles of Morals and Legislation (1789)

Why is it so hard for us to face that our truths are often fantasies? How can Jeremy Bentham, hardly a guy to be riding in the float at the head of the flamboyant, the shocking, and the spit-in-your-eye crowd, still be telling us from the eighteenth century what we don't yet know in the twenty-first?

Normal is about people widely considered not normal: female-to-male transsexuals, heterosexual crossdressers, and the intersexed, sometimes known as hermaphrodites. I originally wrote the first essay, "The Body Lies," for *The New Yorker.* "Isn't there anything you've wondered about and never understood?" Tina Brown, then the editor, asked me.

"Whatever it is, write about that." There was, and is, a long list of such things, but people who had chosen to have traumatizing surgeries to change their gender permanently, and men adamant about desiring both women and their clothes, were at the top of it, since in both cases I could not imagine what kind of people these would be. I didn't know enough about the intersexed even to wonder.

My ignorance was outstripped by my presumptions and assumptions. Surely, transsexuals were either severely delusional and easy prey for unscrupulous doctors, or else they were just victims of our nutty, gender-obsessed society. No, as it turns out. Surely, heterosexual crossdressers were closeted gay men whose innate femininity was expressed through the wearing of women's clothes. No, as it turns out. Surely, those unhappy intersexed people were crazy, even self-destructive, to suggest that intersexed babies were not served by early surgery. No, as it turns out.

It is true, as physicians and scientists and novelists know, that pathology teaches us something about health, as unhappiness teaches us something about happiness and loss teaches us something about what we have. It's also true that there is, in all of these dichotomies, more of a continuum and a mix than we sometimes think.

In spending time with people whose circumstances have forced them to think hard about issues of identity and gender, of the public and the private, in ways that most of us can shrug off if we wish to, I learned as much about our culture's blind spots as about their habits, and as much about the commonality of human needs, no matter how uncommon the costume or the physical package. The female-to-male transsexuals pushed me to think, as I had not, much, about what makes a man, and why, and why we care; the crossdressers, about the nature of marriage and marital happiness and the ties and binds of femininity; the intersexed, about medical practice and its great advances, and great failures, and about the real damage of shame and silence and the process and costs of change.

And all these people became, not the transsexuals, the crossdressers, the intersexed, but Michael and Luis, Dixie and Rebecca, Cheryl and Hale. People. People with stories and wishes and good luck and bad, and as much as their stories are filled with intriguing details and terrible ones, with really funny, and really awful, encounters with the world, they are the stories of people whose hopes and needs, however foreign or familiar, teach us about ourselves as well as about them, and whose difference calls upon the rest of us to examine where the real differences lie.

There are shelves and shelves of academic, clinical, ideological, and autobiographical books on one or more of the subjects I address here. I didn't want to add to them; I wanted to tell the stories of the people I met and how it was to be with them, to offer readers a chance to see what I saw, perhaps to see further and better, and to see into these particular worlds and back out to the larger one we all share.

The names of many of the people in this book, and some identifying details about them, have been altered at their request.

THE BODY LIES

FEMALE-TO-MALE TRANSSEXUALS

What would you go through not to have to live the life of Kafka's Gregor Samsa? Not to realize, early in childhood, that other people perceive a slight, unmistakable bugginess about you, which you find horrifying but they claim to find unremarkable? That glimpses of yourself in the mirror are upsetting and puzzling and to be avoided, since they show a self that is not you? That although you can ignore your shell much of the time and your playmates often seem to see you and not your cockroach exterior, teachers and relatives pluck playfully at your antennae with increasing frequency and suggest, not unkindly, that you might be more comfortable with the other insects? And when you say, or cry, that you are not a cockroach, your parents are sad, or concerned, or annoyed, but unwavering in their conviction—how could it be otherwise?—that you *are* a cockroach, and are becoming more cockroachlike every day. Would you hesitate to pay thirty thousand dollars and experience some sharp but passing physical misery in order to be returned to your own dear, soft, skin-covered self?

Approximately two people in every hundred thousand are diagnosed—first by themselves, then by endocrinologists, family doctors, psychiatrists, or psychologists—as high-intensity transsexuals, meaning that they will be motivated, whether or not they succeed, to have surgery that will bring their bodies into accord with the gender to which they have known themselves, since toddlerhood, to belong. Until a decade or so ago the clinical literature and the unreliable statistics suggested that for every four men seeking to become anatomically female, there was one woman seeking the opposite change. Now clinical evaluation centers report that the ratio is almost one to one.

In twenty years of practice as a clinical social worker, I met men who liked to wear women's clothing, women who preferred sex in public conveyances to sex at home, men who were more attracted to shoes than to the people in them; I didn't meet any transsexuals. I encountered transsexuals only the way most people do: in Renee Richards's story, in Jan Morris's *Conundrum,* in Kate Bornstein's books, and on afternoon talk shows, where transsexuals are usually represented by startlingly pretty young women, sometimes holding hands with their engagingly shy, love-struck fiancés, sometimes accompanied by defensive, supportive wives turned best friends. I wondered, in the middle of the afternoon, where the female-to-male transsexuals were. Even if there were four times as many male-to-female transsexuals, there still had to be a few thousand of the other kind somewhere. But not in mainstream bookstores, not in magazines, not in front of talk-show audiences of middle-aged women standing up to applaud the guests' ability to "look just like the real thing."

I thought there must be a reason female-to-male transsexuals were invisible. I wondered if their physical transformations were so pitiful that no one could bear to interview them, if women who wished to be men were less interesting, less interview-worthy than men who wished to be women, or if these people were so floridly disturbed that even the talk-show hosts were ashamed to be seen with them.

Much of the early psychiatric literature about transsexuals, from the pre–Christine Jorgensen 1940s until the late 1970s, leaned heavily toward psychoanalytic explanations and toward clinical descriptions that, however sympathetic to the unhappy patient, emphasized the bizarreness not of the biological condition but of the conviction that there was a biological condition. The next psychiatric wave emphasized "personality disorders" as the root of transsexuality, specifically the popularized borderline personality syndrome, with its inadequately formed sense of self and frightened yearning for symbiosis. In *The Transsexual Empire* (1979), Janice Raymond dismissed the biological reality of transsexuality and attacked transsexuals as agents and pawns of the patriarchy. Her overwrought theories about the meaning of transsexuality and the training and practice of surgeons who perform transsexual procedures read like the feminist equivalent of some of the Mafia–CIA–White Russian conspiracy theories of Kennedy's assassination, but her essential point, that transsexuals are psychologically unstable victims of a society that overemphasizes the roles of sexual insignia and gender difference, made sense to me. If the people involved were less nuts and society were less rigid, it seemed, neither transsexuals nor the surgery they seek would exist.

Most of us can understand a wish, even a persistent wish, to belong to the other gender. History and fiction are full of examples, many charming, some heroic, of women who dressed as men throughout their lives. It's the medical procedures that make transsexuals seem crazy: six months to two years of biweekly intramuscular injections of two hundred milligrams of Depo-Testosterone, which cause an outbreak of adolescent acne, the cessation of menstruation, and the development of male secondary sex characteristics; then a double mastectomy, in which most but not all of the breast tissue is removed, the nipple saved, and the chest recontoured for a more masculine, pectorally pronounced look; and then, a year to ten years later (depending on the patient's wishes and financial resources), a hysterectomy and one of two possible genital surgeries: a phalloplasty (a surgery to create a full-size phallus and testicles) or a metoidioplasty (a surgery that frees the testosterone-enlarged clitoris to act as a small penis). In short: multiple, expensive, and traumatic surgeries to remove healthy tissue. Who would do this?

Lyle Monelle, a burly man of twenty-eight, lives with his mother, Jessie, in a trailer park in suburban Montana, a state in which I'd never imagined suburbs. The trailer park is neatly laid out beneath a shocking cobalt sky, and all the culs-de-sac have their own blue-and-white street signs, none of which are bent or rusted or facing the wrong way. The careful hand of people who are used to making do, doing without, and trying again is everywhere. Jessie and Lyle are watching for me from the trailer's little porch, and they come toward the car like a couple of welcoming relatives.

The inside of the trailer looks familiar; it is the Montana

twin of my late mother-in-law's home in northern Minnesota. Sturdy, slightly bowed Herculon love seat and matching recliner in shades of orange; copper mallards hanging on the opposite wall, arching over the TV. The three of us finish two pitchers of iced tea during the afternoon's conversation, and Lyle and Jessie allow themselves to be sad and occasionally puzzled by their own story, but not for long. All their painful stories are followed by moments of remembered grief but end in the genuine and ironic laughter of foxhole buddies; they know what they know, and they are not afraid anymore.

Lyle is older than I had thought he would be—he's an adult. He was a patient of three of the people I've already interviewed—Dr. Donald Laub, a preeminent plastic surgeon known especially for female-to-male sex change surgery; Judy Van Maasdam, the counselor at Laub's surgical center in Palo Alto; and Dr. Ira Pauly, a noted psychiatrist—and when they told me about Lyle, they all focused on how young he was at the time of transition, much younger than most people who apply for surgery. Even though I knew better, I had half expected to meet a teenager. He was fourteen when he began hormone treatments, with medical approval, fifteen when he had his mastectomies, but twenty-three before he and his parents had enough money for the phalloplasty, the "bottom" surgery. (That's what the guys say about their surgeries—"my top," "my bottom.") I was horrified when I first heard the stories about this kid, and I imagined meeting his parents and clinically evaluating them as misguided, covertly sadistic, or perversely ignorant, acting out their own unhappiness on their helpless child.

We should all have such parents.

When Lyle entered puberty, his mother and his late father took him from doctor to doctor, looking for explanations for Lyle's unhappiness and fierce resistance to being treated like a young woman. An endocrinologist who had worked with Don Laub recognized Lyle as possibly transsexual, and Ira Pauly and Judy Van Maasdam confirmed the diagnosis. Then, after extensive hormone treatments, Laub performed the first surgery and the family moved to another state, to allow Lyle to enter high school as a boy. Later, they nursed him after his hysterectomy and his phalloplasty, and used all their savings, and then some, to pay his medical bills.

Jessie says, "I want everyone to know who reads this that this wasn't easy—it was a really terrible shock. I didn't understand. I said to the first endocrinologist, 'Where did we go wrong?' and he said nowhere, it was biological. I called every single—I'm not kidding you—every single insurance company in the USA, and they said, 'No, it's cosmetic.' "

Lyle interrupts—the only time I'll see him openly angry. "Yeah, right. Like I wanted a nose job. Cosmetic. Well, it was only my life."

Jessie makes soothing hand gestures, reminding him that it's all right now. "And of course, the money," she says. "Our other kids resented it. I understand. But what could I do? What could we do? If your child has a birth defect, you get help. We understood—we understood even when he was little that something wasn't right. And we knew, when the doctors told us what could be done—we just knew what we had to do. When the doctors said he was transsexual, I felt that I *knew* that."

After hearing Lyle's stories about his hated girl name, his astonished, frightened tears and protracted battles over party dresses, Mary Janes, and even girl-styled polo shirts, and his deep, early sense of male identity—the same stories I would later hear, with minor variations, from almost every transsexual man I spoke with—I ask him about life since the transition. He gives me a glossy friend-filled account highlighted by a two-year romance with an older woman (twenty, to his seventeen) and a successful football career cut short by an ankle injury.

And after high school?

Finally, a bit of trouble: "I had a little money problem and a little drug problem. I got some counseling, came back from Las Vegas, started college. Now I'm taking classes, paying off my bills, working for the state. Eventually, I'll get my bachelor's."

He sighs, and Jessie says quickly, "That's all right. Lots of older kids are in college these days. Aren't they?" I say I know quite a few, and we sip our iced tea.

"I did a lot of partying, some wild times," Lyle continues. "I think maybe I was frustrated. Maybe I did drugs partly because I was so frustrated at not being able to get my bottom surgery right away. Maybe. I just felt not quite right, but the surgery didn't make the difference I thought it would. It just made me feel me—not macho, just *me*. Uh, sexually." He looks at his mother. "It helped me out mentally, not really physically. But it cost so much. Not that Don Laub wasn't fair—he was. And when it was over, all I wanted to say was, 'Thank you, Dr. Laub, for letting me be reborn.' But if it hadn't been for that I'd have a very nice house by now."

He laughs and Jessie laughs. "Me too," she says. "We'd have two very nice houses." Not looking at him, she goes on. "There is another surgery he could have, to get all the feeling"—a surgery in which a nerve taken from the forearm is run through the phallus—"but we just don't have the money."

I didn't ask any questions, because at the time I didn't know much about the different kinds of phalloplasties and I thought that it was rude to ask people about the working condition of their genitals, constructed or otherwise.

Lyle says, "What does it cost? Another forty grand? To have more sensation? It'd be nice, I guess, but I'd rather pay off my debts and buy a condo. What I have is fine. I need to get back on my feet financially and own my home more than I need to—" He laughs again and looks at his mother, who laughs too.

"And anyway," Jessie says, "he wouldn't ever let us see it, even after we nursed him following the surgery."

"Did you want to?" I ask.

Lyle is laughing and shaking his head no.

"Well, yes," Jessie says, slightly injured. "He's my son. I wanted to know."

"No, Mom. I'm twenty-eight. I maintain the boundaries here," Lyle says to me, and his mother smiles, a little puzzled and hurt that this is the thing he won't share.

"I'm pretty darn happy now. I want to finish school, and when I'm ready I'd like to marry, have a family. I'm not ready yet for a serious relationship. Psychologically, I'm just getting ready to date again."

He sounds like a lot of the young men in AA or NA, a little ashamed, a little proud of his hell-raising days, understanding that it's time to grow up, and a little sorry that's so.

We take a break, and Lyle shows me the photographs I've asked to see. It seems absurd to describe the child I'm looking at as a little girl; even in a ruffled blouse, this is a little boy: a sturdy little boy looking adoringly at his dad while happily playing with his electric train, and then a cocky kid in cowboy hat and boots, and then a handsome, shaggy graduating senior being kissed by a pretty girl, and then Lyle as he is now, a friendly, beefy man with thinning blond hair—exactly the look of many West Coast high school football stars ten years down the road.

James Green, a transsexual man who has organized a get-together for me at his Oakland condo, sits beside me in the rental car while I look for the dimmer switch. I'm parked in his parking space, since he has chivalrously moved his car a block away to make room for me. I find the headlights, I find the interior light. I find the wipers. I cannot turn off the brights. James reaches across me with his left hand and adjusts the dimmer switch. The brights go down, and he looks at me exactly as other men have on such occasions: affectionate, pleased, a little charmed by this blind spot of mine. We smile at each other and I shrug. He shrugs too. "It's innate," he says, and he laughs, not taking his eyes off me.

We are dining unfashionably early, in an austerely hip neighborhood café, before the other men arrive at James's place. A huge plate of food is put before James, and he hunches over slightly and begins eating. I notice that he does not say, "Gee, this is a lot of food," or anything of the kind. Like a man, he just starts eating. I ask him how he met the girlfriend he'd mentioned earlier.

James puts his fork down and gives me the full effect of his green eyes. "She's a writer. She was interviewing me." A quick unfolding of a Jack Nicholson smile, and then, with slow mock-shyness, he goes back to his dinner. I smile too.

After dinner, we drive to his condo, which is clearly the home of a writer and a noncustodial father: eclectic reference books spill off the bookshelves, the refrigerator door is bedecked with drawings by and photographs of a cute little girl, dolls and coloring books make a pink-and-purple jumble in a corner of the living room. When James was a lesbian, the woman he lived with had a child, whom he regards as his daughter; after his surgery, they broke up, but he now sees the little girl as much as he can.

The doorbell rings, and James introduces me to Loren and Luis, guys from the local transsexual community.

Loren Cameron, a blond bantamweight photographer, is wearing a billowing tank top and black shorts. He has a tight, perfect build, and startling black stripes tattooed across his chest, on both forearms, and on his thighs. A cross between Mercury and Rob Lowe, he looks like a not uncommon type of handsome, hairless, possibly gay man one sees on beaches and boardwalks.

Loren has been romantically involved with a massage therapist named Elizabeth for the last six years. When I speak to her later, I'm not surprised to learn that she is a former dancer and a fitness fanatic, and to find out for myself that she is marvelously, mellowly narcissistic.

"Well, Loren and I *are* a striking-looking couple," Elizabeth says. "We're both very fit, and I know that people look at us when we walk down the street. After all, I'm about four inches taller than he is." Elizabeth describes her two previous lovers: a beautiful Amazon and an unusually sensitive man. "But with Loren, he can communicate, for the most part, like a woman, and he makes love like a man. When I met him, he was a very attractive woman. Now he's an even more attractive man. And that's that."

Luis is a slightly built, gentle South American man, a chemist in Silicon Valley, thirty-five years old, single and bisexual, primarily involved with women.

"I was twenty-two when I went to Don Laub for my surgery," Luis says. "It was the right thing for me—I can go to the gym, go swimming, and I don't have to feel vulnerable or be afraid. I was always athletic, and I didn't want to give that up. And it feels right for sex. What I perceive and what my partner perceives now match up. Inside and outside, I'm a man.

"The surgeries made a huge difference for me. I had the genital surgery, not the full phalloplasty. I don't know what Dr. Laub calls the other one now, but that's what I had. The easier one [the metoidioplasty]. I have days when I think about a phalloplasty, but I'd rather save my money, for travel, for my future, for investing. The gender issue isn't at the center of my life." He sighs.

"I don't get the chance to talk about this, it's not a conversation I'd have with other men. Gender is slippery. I used to see it as black and white—men, women, that's it. I wanted to be perceived as male, in a male role, with male attributes. I don't hold on to that anymore. Male, female—I don't even understand that anymore. Now that I've been in a female body and in a male one and spent all this time thinking about this issue, I see that it's nebulous. You can't hold on to it and find meaning. Gender is an illusion, an illusion we cherish because we think we'll ultimately find something clear and meaningful. And we don't, we won't. And I find, after all this, it doesn't matter much."

The four of us talk for two hours, and Loren and James cheerfully interrupt each other, disagreeing, raising their voices, picking holes in each other's logic; Luis and I listen, and from time to time we point out the issues on which James and Loren do agree, which seems to matter to us but not to them.

They agree—they both know at first hand—that a number of transsexual men have emerged from the lesbian community, a world in which each of them could maneuver with some success but not with complete ease. "I was excluded from lesbian events even before I started the transition," James says. "I was just too male—not butch but male. I crossed some line somehow, and everyone, the other women, felt that there were things about me, despite my female body, that were just not female."

Loren, apparently irritated by James's calm, even superior acquiescence to rejection by the community that was their world for so many years, adds, "The loss makes me mad, losing the women's community. And the lack of acknowledgment. Transsexuals are never really accepted, by anyone."

Luis says, very quietly, reluctant to antagonize the activists, "I'm not really very political. I take calculated risks, I do a little public speaking. I have a lot of other things I like to do and develop besides politics. My parents are apolitical, my whole family is. I'm not a separatist, of any kind. I find separatism ugly. I understand straight men at least as well as I understand gay women. I used to hate and fear men, at least all the ones I knew. Now I don't. Probably you don't have to become anatomically male to stop hating men." He smiles. "But it is effective. I can now meet men that I can trust, I can care for."

And his view of women?

"I was like a fly on the wall in my childhood world of girls. I grew up with girls, in their world, and I saw how they were treated. I didn't feel like one of them, but I saw how women were disrespected, were diminished, and I haven't forgotten that."

We wind up talking about Virginia Woolf's *Orlando* and weightlifting and fathers and children and photography. I like these men, and I know, whatever "knowing" means, that they're men. I expected to find psychologically disturbed, male-identified women so filled with self-loathing that it had even spilled onto their physical selves, leading them to self-mutilating, self-punishing surgery. Maybe I would meet some very butch lesbians, in ties and jackets and chest binders, who could not, somehow, accept their female bodies. I didn't meet those people. I met men. Some I liked, some I didn't. I met bullshit artists, salesmen, computer programmers, compulsive, misogynistic seducers, pretty boys inviting seduction, cowboys, New Age prophets, good ol' boys, shy truck drivers saving their money for a June wedding, and gentle knights. I met men.

Ira Pauly is one of the acknowledged titans of transsexual psychiatry. He is professor emeritus and former chairman of the department of psychiatry at the University of Nevada School of Medicine. In his bunkerlike office at the university, he cautions me that he hasn't kept up with everything in the recent literature, which represents a huge body of work and new ideas. He says that he has met a few people who have had regrets after their surgery, but only a few, out of hundreds, and that whatever the etiology of transsexuality may be, there are those for whom surgery is the only true solution.

Pauly is a modest, very smart man with big hands and a UCLA plaque on his desk showing his college football history. He became chairman of the department of psychiatry partly on the strength of his pioneering research on transsexuals. He is always clear, reasonable, fair, and extremely contained. He showed strong feeling only once during our interview—when he talked about Louis Sullivan.

A female-to-male transsexual, Sullivan was also a gay man with AIDS, and he called Pauly in the late eighties in the hope of educating the professionals in the "gender community" about the difference between gender and sexual orientation: that a "real" man might prefer sex with men to sex with women; that the sexual object one prefers says nothing at all about one's gender, or even about one's masculinity or femininity. Sullivan encountered massive resistance, even from physicians and mental health professionals who regularly supervised and facilitated transsexual transitions. "But if you want to sleep with a man," they said, in effect, "why not go on being a woman? It's so easy." As if only a nutty transsexual would believe that sex with a man, as a man, is different from sex with a man, as a woman.

In his search for treatment, Sullivan went to several gender dysphoria clinics ("gender dysphoria" meaning that the presenting complaint is one of deep unhappiness with one's gender). For transsexuals, Ira Pauly told me, such clinics are the only gateways to reputable surgeons committed to meaningful standards of care: under the supervision of a clinic, the patient lives full-time as a member of the opposite sex for two years before surgery and receives documented treatment by a licensed mental health practitioner (the process recommended by the Harry Benjamin International Gender Dysphoria Association, an organization of gender dysphoria professionals—psychologists, social workers, psychiatrists, surgeons, endocrinologists, the occasional lawyer). Sullivan was rejected by the clinics because he not only knew that despite his female anatomy he was male, he knew that he was a gay male.

Pauly loaned me three hours of videotaped interviews he had conducted with Sullivan. The setup reminded me of public access TV: a ficus tree keeps brushing Sullivan's ears, the carpeting clashes with the chairs, the camera occasionally seems stuck on the sock sliding down Ira Pauly's bare shin or on Louis Sullivan's pale hands fumbling with the mike. If you missed the sections on surgery and hormones, you would simply be moved by this increasingly gaunt, youngish, mild-mannered man so ferociously determined to make use of his AIDS death sentence to educate the rest of us.

"They said, 'It can't be,' and I said, 'It is,'" Sullivan says on one of the tapes. "They told me that I must not really be transsexual. After all, they thought, if I just wanted to sleep with men, why go to all the trouble? So, I told them. Again and again, until they got it."

The notion that gender has a continuum, a fluid range of possibilities, seems to produce such anxious rigidity in many of us that we ignore everything we've learned through our own lives about the complexities of men and women, and seek refuge in explanations and expectations of gender that are more magical, romantic, and unrealistic than any attitude I encountered among the transsexuals I met. Ever since Christine Jorgensen, there seems to have been a lot of confusion about what now, thanks to Louis Sullivan, seems so unconfused to Ira Pauly and others in the field. Male is not gay or straight; it's male. We may not know what it is, but we know it's not about whether male or female sexual stimuli inspire your erection. Maybe it's not even about the ability or the equipment to have an erection. Maybe it's closer to the sensation of inner arousal pushed out—a sense of erectness, of intact outerness—than to the source or object of one's erotic desires. There are gay men, heterosexual men, bisexual men, masculine men, feminine men. We know that neither the object of desire nor the drinking of beer nor the clenching of fists makes maleness. We don't know what does, and neither do the transsexual men, and neither do the people who treat them, psychologically and surgically.

I ask Dr. Pauly, who has expressed caution about the usefulness of transsexual surgery—and even more caution about those psychiatrists who wish to have the surgery declared a problem rather than a solution—if he would recommend surgery if he had a transsexual child.

"I would hope not to have a transsexual child; that life is no easy thing, with or without the surgery. I *hope* that the follow-up studies support the studies we have now. I *hope* these patients are happier."

I press him.

"I would probably try to intervene early in childhood. But you know, those studies of strongly effeminate boys—a lot of them grow up to be gay, but they don't grow up to be transsexual. You're looking at five in a hundred for male homosexuals, one in fifty thousand for transsexuals."

In the end, after edging up on saying that he would advise surgery if he had a transsexual child, Dr. Pauly shrugs and nods yes but doesn't say it, and I stop. There is some kind of gift in having been in both a male and a female body in one lifetime, but it is not a gift anyone wants for their child.

At Don Laub's surgical center in Palo Alto, I stand in the doorway of the waiting room, observing two women in the courtyard, wondering if they are "genetically female," and wondering if I can bring myself to ask such a rude question. But if I believe, as I now find myself believing, that transsexual men and women are men and women, what would make the question rude? The implication that something tipped me off, that their femininity was imperfect, that there was some trace of the masculine in their appearance? I have been noticing traces of the imperfect, traces of the other gender in people, for two days now, ever since I met with Lyle and Jessie and with the guys at James's condo.

The person on the side of the courtyard nearest me is blond, pretty, curvy, lightly made up in suitable-for-blonds colors. Conservative navy dress, white trim. Suntan hose and navy pumps. Could be, I think. Good makeup, but maybe just a bit stereotypically feminine, maybe a little overboard. She gestures to her companion forcefully, and I think, Ah, those hands. Very strong, even at a distance. I look at the companion. Thin and angular, in loose black pants and a loose black-and-ivory shirt. No visible curves at all. Reddish wavy hair gathered back tightly from a long, shining, intense, and makeupless face. But the narrowness of the forehead, the size and shape and prominence of the eyes. I don't think so. And she laughs, showing her braces, and I think, Can't be. This red-haired person, although not particularly feminine or womanly, is a genetic female.

I go into the courtyard, and the blond calls my name and introduces herself: Dr. Gail Lebovic, Dr. Laub's associate. She introduces me to Selena, a visiting medical student. We sit in the courtyard a while longer, waiting for Don Laub, and I watch for tall, big-handed women, short, wide-hipped men with scraggly facial hair. A broad-shouldered, pot-bellied woman with a bad dye job comes through the courtyard, bandy-legged and squat. The cleaning lady. Genetic female. There's a slim, wispy-mustached young man in the corridor. Sean, the new office worker. Genetic male.

We are joined by Dr. Laub, graying and clean-shaven, utterly conventional and conservative in a dark-suited, rep-tie way, except for eyes so brightly intense they seem silver rather than blue-gray. He went to Jesuit schools, has been married forever to the same woman, and has five children, one of whom is a microsurgeon in Vermont, and one a registered nurse. He is also the founder of Interplast, a charitable organization that sends plastic surgeons to poor countries to provide free corrective surgery for children and adults. As of this writing, Laub's center has done 798 female-to-male surgeries, most performed by Laub himself before he retired in 2001. Of that number, two female-to-male transsexuals asked to have their phalloplasties reversed and to return to female bodies. Although both reported that they were happy in their lives as men, they had become born-again Christians, and had been advised that their sex change surgeries were not God's will.

Don Laub and Gail Lebovic show me some photograph albums of their female-to-male patients—dozens of head shots, before, during, and after hormone treatments. It begins to seem to me that what we take as the immutable biological fact of our existence is, after all, largely hormonal and unnervingly fluid. Many of the pictures of the same patient at various stages of his transformation look like family portraits—younger, middle, and eldest brother. The faces broaden; the foreheads slope forward and down more roughly to the eyebrows from receding hairlines; the necks and shoulders widen. Strength training is recommended for female-to-male transsexuals, to deal with the weight gain, but many of the men in the photographs are somewhere between stocky and fat. A few of them are handsome, more than a few are attractive, most are average. One guy looks like Don Ho, another looks like Don Knotts, another like Richard Gere. Some are homely, with bad skin, bad haircuts, cheap eyeglasses and overwashed shirts, ugly mustaches, pouchy eyes, jowly necks. But no one in his right mind would take them for women.

Lebovic clears her throat and shows me the other pictures. I've seen them before, the pictures Don Laub sent me of phalloplasties and metoidioplasties; I flipped through them at home and tried to study them, but they were black-and-white photocopies. The originals are in brutal, Polaroid-type color, in which brown skin has a dappled, froglike quality, and white skin has the sheen and color of bad pork.

Lebovic occasionally points out items of interest. "See,

with this surgery"—the phalloplasty—"we keep the clitoris. Here, underneath, just above the scrotum, so when the penis is either rubbing against it or pulled out of the way, there's full sexual response. Isn't that great? We make the scrotum with the labia, by inserting skin expanders, just a little bit, week by week. After the skin has expanded, we insert the testicular implants, stitch it up the middle a bit, to create the look. Otherwise you just have one big ball, like this. Picture a small deflated balloon—that's the expander. We put one in each labium, sew the labia together, and expand each compartment so it's just like testicles. Then we put in the implants, just silicone balls."

She describes the painful electrolysis of the abdominal area (all hair must be removed from the skin that will be used to make the phallus), and then the surgery. Two vertical incisions are made, three inches apart, stopping short of the navel. The surgeon lifts up the skin and soft tissue while it's still attached at the ends, and rolls it up lengthwise into a tube. This inside-out tube is covered with a skin graft from the hip. The soft, skin-covered tube is still attached in two places, at the navel and the bikini line, and will be left that way, a pulsing hot dog growing on the abdominal field, for at least three months, so that it will develop its own blood supply. The second stage requires detaching the tube at the navel end and allowing the newly developed phallus to drop down. Function, of course, in the form of urination and ejaculation, is another matter. Urination through the phallus can be arranged, but the production and ejaculation of sperm is not yet possible.

The photograph Don Laub shows me next must be a picture of something gone wrong. Underneath the penis is a huge, brownish, fuzzy red ball, a little bigger than a tennis ball. Nothing wrong, Lebovic says a little dubiously, it must just be a fresh post-op. Laub reassures me later that there wasn't anything wrong in the case, just something a little unusual.

"This was a very macho Mexican guy, and he felt that he really needed it—them—to be big, so I expanded the labia way out so the scrotum would hang properly large."

We come to some terrible pictures. These are of men, genetic men, who've had penises created after disease or trauma. "Burn, cancer, tree shredder," Lebovic says gently.

Next we look at an album of various completed phalloplasties, which is much easier than looking at the squirming reds and yellows and acres of flaccid, anesthetized skin in the surgical procedures used to construct them. The penises here are long, blobby tubes with no real heads, no color.

"These are the early ones," Lebovic says. "You see the shape is not so great. And of course, Dr. Laub was making them huge. I mean, really." She shows me a photograph with a ruler held up to the penis. I'm reluctant to lean closer to read the number of inches. "Nine," she says, laughing. "Well, Dr. Laub is a guy. I guess he figured that if you want one, you may as well get a big one. Now they're a little closer to average. And there's no erectile tissue, so you wouldn't want it too small."

The penises are starting to look more familiar, more penis-like. I'm getting used to the black, hard-looking stitches. The guys in the photo album are predominantly white, but transsexuals come in every ethnic and racial group.

On to the metoidioplasties—a surgery sometimes called clitoral release. These penises look, just as Laub's articles say they do, like the penises of small boys, or like "what you'd see in a men's locker room on a chilly day," as he writes. "I don't really understand why anyone has this surgery," Lebovic says. "I mean, if you're going to have a penis . . ."

She flips back to the first photo album and points to a WASPy middle-aged businessman with the silver flattop I associate with California Rotarians.

"He was my first. I had just come over from Stanford to spend time with Dr. Laub. Reconstructive breast surgery was my strong interest, and he's incredibly good at that. He says to me, 'How do you feel about working with transsexuals?' And I said, 'Oh, fine.' Because I had no idea—I went to Berkeley, I figure I'm open-minded, it'll be all right. Dr. Laub points me to one of the examining rooms, and I go in and find a middle-aged couple. I don't even know who the patient is, but I look at the chart and I see it's him. I ask him how he's doing, he says, 'Not too bad,' and I'm trying to make an educated guess, to figure out what's wrong, what kind of cosmetic surgery he's here for. Finally I ask him, 'Have you had any previous surgeries?' and he says, 'Why, yes, the double mastectomy and the hysterectomy.' And I thought, But you're a *man*. People outside the field always say, 'He, she, whatever,' in that tone of voice, you know the tone I mean. But that question never arises once you meet them, once you open yourself up to the danger."

What danger?

"The danger of questioning everything we take for granted. The danger of questioning yourself."

I arrange to meet Don Laub again in New York City, at the Harry Benjamin International Gender Dysphoria Symposium. Harry Benjamin came from Germany in 1913 to do his residency in endocrinology; he stayed in America and began a private practice, pursuing his fascination with the aging process and the study of glands. Alfred Kinsey, wanting an endocrinological assessment of a puzzling young man, sent Benjamin his first transsexual patient, in 1948, and changed the focus of Benjamin's career. In 1966 Benjamin published *The Transsexual Phenomenon,* still widely used as a reference. He was, by all reports, the most lovable of men. He retired at ninety and died in 1986 at a hundred and one.

I haven't yet understood the mechanics of all the intricate surgical procedures, and at my request Laub is going to explain them to me again. The conference is being held at the Marriott Marquis Hotel, and we sit down at a little table in a corridor that also functions as a lounge. Laub demonstrates the various genital surgeries for female-to-male transsexuals on lined yellow paper, using his pen point as a scalpel.

The four options are the basic phalloplasty, with external devices for erection and urination; two deluxe models, both of which provide the capacity to urinate in the typical male position (one also affords some physical sensation); and the metoidioplasty. All four are major surgeries, with more than one step. Mastectomies almost always precede the genital surgeries, which include hysterectomies and testicular implants.

Before long, Laub and I are surrounded by large and small yellow penises and one Red Grooms–style paper sculpture, with which Laub has walked me through three stages of the deluxe phalloplasty that includes the removal of a nerve from the forearm and its placement within the newly created phallus, running from the glans of the new penis to the nerves of the still existing clitoris and allowing a full range of sensation.

"I call this the postmodern one. Like those buildings over there." He waves vaguely toward the newer architecture of Times Square.

I've heard transsexual patients and others—especially Stanley Biber, the grandfather-king of male-to-female surgery—talk about the horrifying scarring of the forearm when the skin and nerve are used to make the tube for the phallus. Laub shows me just how much of the forearm is taken for the standard flap, and I cringe as he runs his pen over most of the underside of my arm.

"I don't do the standard flap. The goal is always, in surgery, the least 'expensive,' meaning least traumatic, donor site." He describes stretching the thin, hairless skin of the forearm with tissue expanders so that when the skin and nerve and an artery are removed there's only a thin incision, nothing worse. "It's less than two inches across," he assures me, "and then you've got urinary function and sensitivity. I got tired of other people making presentations, and showing the basic phalloplasty with the baculum [one of the devices used to maintain erections] and the urinary assist device, and saying, 'Well, here's the traditional method, as used by Don Laub.' That's still the one most patients choose. It's functional, it's much less expensive, in both senses, and you don't burn any bridges. I've done about a hundred and fifty of those. A hundred and forty-eight. You can always go back and reconstruct at a later date."

Including the mastectomy, the whole procedure for the basic sex change surgery costs twenty thousand dollars; if your insurance company is persuaded that you truly have the psychiatric disorder of transsexualism, for which surgery is a necessary part of the treatment, you might get reimbursement from them—after you've agreed to go through life with an official diagnosis probably comparable in many people's minds to necrophilia. The prices at Laub's surgical center haven't gone up for years, and are a little lower than those of some other surgeons, including many who are still learning the techniques.

"This other kind of phalloplasty, which allows for natural, unassisted urination, calls for a year of electrolysis in a very sensitive place, the pubic region and lower stomach. And sometimes even then the hair grows back. But you see"—he quickly makes an incision in the paper and rolls up the tube—"you can't have urination through the tunnel if there's hair. The skin has to be hairless, so you either have to find hairless skin"—he taps my forearm—"or make it."

He draws a long spoon. "With the first kind of phalloplasty, the one I've done the most often, this [urinary assist] device is what they use. You slip it in from the meatus [the opening for urination] right through the phallus. It's very soft, flexible plastic. And after all, in men's bathrooms, men are like this." Don Laub stands up, hand placed over his belt buckle, and stares ahead with slight trepidation. His eyes dart from left to right and then fasten on the opposite wall. "The norm is not to look. With peripheral vision, all they're going to see is some guy fumbling with his shorts and then urinating. That's all. It works.

"Now, the metoidioplasty—it's from *meta,* meaning 'toward,' *oidio,* for the male genitals, and *plasty,* 'change.' " He draws and dissects another set of female genitalia, carving out a small penis and folding over the lips of the labia majora to make a very neat, actually rather cute scrotum. "I don't think the patients really prefer this—I mean, if money were no object. Maybe some, some who are not such high-intensity transsexuals. Sometimes their wives don't want the penises—they've been married eight, ten years, and I'm showing them the choices. I sit there like an encyclopedia salesman, showing them the different models, and maybe the wife says, 'We want the metoidioplasty.' And the husband says, 'We do? I don't think so, honey. I want the phalloplasty.' And that relationship is in trouble. Because, for the most part—again, if money's no object and this is a younger man—he wants a penis. Men want penises. But the metoidioplasty mimics nature, and that's appealing. The testosterone enlarges the clitoris. It's the way men and women both are in utero—an enlarged clitoris, which does or doesn't become a penis. And it's one-stage surgery, less expensive than the other, and obviously sexual and urinary functioning is intact and they can go on having sex however they had it. Like lesbians do."

"You mean sex without intercourse? That's all that they don't get, right? No penile penetration."

Laub pauses. "Well, yes. It's only about an inch and a half, maybe two inches. So they can go on having the kind of sex they had before. Dildos, whatever."

Laub next describes the four different devices that allow the men to have erections (a minority of those who have the forearm flap surgery won't even need a device). The devices fall into two categories: pumps and inserts. One pump, the most discreet, is small, ball-like, and implanted in the scrotum. When activated, it pumps fluid from inside the ball into the penis, which remains erect for about ten minutes. There is also a syringelike external pump, which is attached to a condom. When activated, the pump evacuates the air from the hollow tube of the penis, forming a vacuum within it and hardening the outer casing—"like making Styrofoam," Laub says. Of the two inserts, one is permanent, and the other is used only as needed. Laub is wary of the permanent implant, a woven silver-wire tube within a silicone sheath, which gives the penis some rigidity, whether pointed up or down. "It's dangerous to have implants where you have no feeling," Laub says. He recommends the baculum, slightly thicker than a ballpoint pen, coated with Teflon, and tailor-made, rather inexpensively, for each patient. It is inserted before intercourse, extends from the tip of the penis back to the clitoris, and allows for tireless intercourse and full sensation from the pressure on the clitoris, now located above the scrotum.

Laub is more comfortable with the men who choose penises and intercourse and who have clear-cut, easily identifiable heterosexual preferences, but he not only does the metoidioplasties, he does them extremely well and teaches other surgeons to do them. Still, as is so commonly the case in the medical world, the doctors and the patients involved in these procedures often understand their relationships in radically different ways. The doctors are trained to believe that they know, not only how, but also what and why and for whom. Patients, whether they have breast cancer or AIDS or colds, often want to be active partners in a treatment process marked by dialogue and exploration. At worst, patients see doctors as arrogant technicians; doctors see patients as self-endangering fools. Many of the men I interviewed preferred metoidioplasties, but never for the reasons offered in the literature or by the surgeons. The gender professionals say that patients choose metoidioplasties because they're older and don't want to go through the more complicated surgery, or because they have other medical conditions that contraindicate surgery, or because they were lesbians before transition and their partners don't like the idea of sex with a man (as though if your partner had a beard, a deep voice, and no breasts, you would think you were in bed with a woman). But every transsexual man I spoke to who'd chosen metoidioplasty said, in essence, "I don't need a big, expensive penis;

this little one does just fine, and I can use the money to enhance my life." It was like interviewing a bunch of proud and content but slightly bewildered Volkswagen owners and, across town, some slightly miffed and equally bewildered Mercedes dealers.

James Green said, "I chose this because, well, I don't really feel the need for a big one and I like having the range of feeling I always did. This form of sexual pleasure is fine for me and for my girlfriend. And the other costs a lot of money. A *lot* of money."

Loren Cameron said, "It's not all or nothing. I can live this way, as a man with a vagina. If I could get a fully functioning penis, I'd have the surgery. But I'm not prepared to go through more surgery, all of these procedures, to wind up with a pair of plastic testicles and not much more. I know who I am."

I don't think the idea of a man choosing to keep his vagina would make sense to Don Laub, although Loren would never find a more skillful or compassionate surgeon.

During the Harry Benjamin symposium, I talk to other doctors besides Laub, and to psychologists, psychiatrists, even psychoanalysts, people who collectively have worked with a thousand transsexuals and their families, in the United States and in northern Europe. Among them is Dr. Leah Schaefer, who is a psychologist, a genetic female, and a past president of the Harry Benjamin Association, and has treated hundreds of people like Loren, James, Luis, and Lyle. She is small and rounded, the right kind of Mitteleuropa figure for full skirts, big belts, and a lace fichu at the neck. We meet at her Manhattan office, which is in her home and is itself homey, *haimish*—dried flowers, ceramic birds, carved boxes, family photographs, and a little sculpture of an Orthodox Jewish man studying Torah. I didn't expect the mezuzah on the doorway, or that she would have spent twelve years singing professionally, or that we would end up talking about her closetful of shoes, talking with the same shared enthusiasm and tenderness you hear in the voices of boat enthusiasts, golfers, and transsexuals comparing surgical work.

"There are probably more than five thousand postoperative transsexuals in the United States now. You have small-town surgeons setting up shop just like the well-known ones, the ones with years of training. I've seen over five hundred people, but no researchers have ever interviewed me or asked for my statistics when they're gathering information. There's not a good statistics bank here in America. I'm afraid I don't know where people get their numbers."

Later, she brightens when she thinks of "a very wonderful scientist" to tell me about.

"Friedemann Pfafflin's everything—an M.D., a psychoanalyst, a practicing clinician. He has a better vantage point than a lot of researchers. He's just wonderful."

And he's in New York, it happens, attending the symposium. The first thing on Dr. Pfafflin's mind when I meet with him and Peggy Cohen-Kettenis, a Dutch clinical psychologist who knows him well and has suggested a joint interview, is where he can smoke.

"It's amazing," he says. "In America I don't feel like a smoker, I feel like a murderer."

I assure him that I don't mind smoking, and we go to my hotel room, but he doesn't smoke there either, because there are no ashtrays.

Dr. Pfafflin absolutely knows where he gets his numbers. He doesn't seem to think much of American record-keeping, but he has found the data banks in Germany, the Netherlands, Australia, and Sweden to be reliable, and has been doing research and follow-up studies for the last twenty years. He shows me two studies. The first is based on the Bem Sex Role Inventory, a psychological test, oriented differently for men and women, to assess feelings of masculinity and femininity; one of its underlying assumptions is that a mix of masculine and feminine is normal and healthy in both males and females. The study compares female-to-male (FTM) transsexuals, before and after hormonal and/or surgical treatment, with "normal"—that is, genetic—females. The transsexuals test out as high masculine/low feminine before the treatment, and afterward as well-adjusted men who accept their feminine side.

The second study, based on a German psychological test similar to the Minnesota Multiphasic Personality Inventory (a psychological personality evaluation widely used in the gender dysphoria clinics here), has even broader implications. The FTM transsexuals are compared with normal men and with normal women, and I don't need to read German to understand the charts: they are as clear as cartoons. The good-sized gray bar down the middle is normal men on page one, normal women on page two; green lines that run in and out of the gray bars are the untreated transsexuals, and red lines that run square in the center of the male page and close to the middle on the female page are the post-op transsexuals. "They are completely in the normal range, psychologically, for men, after treatment," Pfafflin says, running his finger up and down the gray bar. "Even before treatment, they are not so off the norm for women" (which suggests, unpleasantly, that the norm for women contains a fair amount of depression and low self-esteem). Pfafflin also mentions other clinical and research studies showing no unusual levels of psychopathology in the families of transsexual teenagers or in the adolescents themselves.

Neither Pfafflin nor Cohen-Kettenis appears to be particularly impressed by the surgeons in their field. Cohen-Kettenis, consistently more tactful, shrugs slightly when I ask about the exchange of ideas between the surgeons and the mental health people here at the conference. Pfafflin laughs. "Well, they are naïve, like children. They love to build. I will build a little clitoris, I will build a little penis."

Cohen-Kettenis smiles. "Not a little penis. Only big ones."

Although they attend the surgeons' presentations (ten to twenty minutes of endless, blurring slides of penises and vaginas and recontoured chests and abdominal flaps and forearm donor sites and Y-shaped incisions), they don't expect the surgeons to attend the psychological presentations. Laub has told me that the surgeons do. He does.

Cohen-Kettenis says, "We need to know about the surgery for our patients, to provide information. The surgeons don't need to know what we do, or think."

"And they wouldn't understand," Pfafflin says, and then corrects himself, perhaps remembering that his colleagues might read this. "Some of them wouldn't. Anyway, they have their psychologists and so on screening the patients for them, so they don't need to know."

When I find Don Laub again, in a meeting room filled with energetic, well-dressed men and women whose genetic origins are impossible to know, I ask him about the root of high-intensity transsexuality, the kind for which surgery seems to be the only solution. "I believe it's biological and behavioral," he says. "A behavioral problem with a surgical solution. There have been a number of experiments, corroborated over and over, at Wisconsin, at Oregon, at Stanford. They injected lab mammals—cats, rats, dogs, and monkeys—with opposite-sex hormones shortly before birth. And that was it. No matter what kind of conditioning you used on those mammals, they behaved consistently like the opposite sex, like the gender of the hormone with which they were injected. And I think that that's what we'll find, eventually: a biological answer.

"Of course, we're the true believers here. We know we're right. I've been doing Interplast for years now, and it's taken off, people understand, they give money to it. But with this, with gender dysphoria, people still don't get it, they don't accept it. For twenty-five years I've been doing this work, and the only people who really understand it are all at this meeting. Or they're the patients. When plastic surgeons begin doing this work, a lot of them just see the technical challenge, the professional opportunity. They dislike the whole idea of transsexuals, but they're fascinated by the challenge. But when they meet the patients, they change—they become more empathetic. They see the people and they are forever changed.

"You know, this is the ultimate body-image surgery. And if people are fundamentally at peace with themselves, like any other cosmetic surgery, they're likely to have a good outcome. I've learned from my gender patients: I screen my cosmetic patients better now. A forty-five-year-old woman with small breasts, whose real agenda is to have breast augmentation because her husband works for an international corporation and when he's on the road he takes out every big-busted lady he can find—she's not a good candidate. After she's happy, after she's worked out her marriage, then she's a good candidate, if that's what she wants. These gender patients, they cross-live, they have therapy, they're evaluated over and over. By the time they have the surgery, they're successful economically, socially, psychologically, usually sexually too. Those are good candidates for plastic surgery. And that's how the other patients should be too, but we don't usually do that kind of screening, we don't expect it of the patient or of the surgeon."

I ask Laub what developments he anticipates in his field.

"The future has three parts," he says. "FTM surgery's going to improve, aesthetically and in other ways. I learned something here at the conference. I'm going to start doing it right away. They showed how to construct the glans, how to build up a corona. I'll start doing that. And they tattoo a pinkish color onto the head—that helps too. I'm going to do that. And in the future there might be transplants, if we can figure out how to reduce rejection. I don't think the government will fund penis transplants, but we'll try to persuade it to. And there's the chemical approach, trying to prevent problems, handling tissue receptors differently, correcting. And then we come back to surgery, and we keep trying to make it better. Because that's what the patients need, and that's what we strive for: the best anatomical solution to the problem, since the problem has no other solution."

Until fairly recently, pragmatic, solution-oriented approaches like Don Laub's were anathema to clinical theorists, whose diagnoses and suggestions for treatment focused primarily on male-to-female transsexuals and on the inevitable opinions about preexisting family pathology. Absent fathers, overinvolved mothers—that was the traditional psychoanalytic explanation for male homosexuality, and for transsexuality as well, though some clinicians have taken the opposite view: dominant fathers, submissive mothers. The other two major psychological theories are that parents of transsexuals encourage cross-gender identification and play, and that parents of transsexuals strongly discourage cross-gender identification and play. That about covers it. I can't imagine that with the dominant and absent fathers, the passive and active mothers, and the encouraging and discouraging of cross-gender behaviors, we've left out too many American families (except the single parents, and they have their own problems). According to these theories, there should be millions of transsexuals in America alone, and McSurgery centers in every good-sized town.

No one cares at all about theory at what I'll call the American Fantasia conference. It's a big get-together of crossdressing men and their wives and a smaller group of transsexual men and women and their partners, held behind a homemade curtain of pink tablecloths, down the most remote corridor of a smallish motel in a Southern suburb.

American Fantasia is organized by a man whose name I can't use: although many at the gathering know that he's transsexual, his neighbors don't, his colleagues don't, the psychiatrists and psychologists and social workers to whom he regularly lectures on transsexuality don't. I don't know either, until he tells me, halfway through the interview. In his earnest, slightly old-fashioned suit, with his tidy hair and beard, he looks like a behavioral psychologist or a very effective insurance salesman. He has a deep, manly chuckle that gets on my nerves, especially when it punctuates his belittling remarks about male-to-female crossdressers and the amusement with which female-to-male transsexuals regard them. I'm annoyed until I realize, with surprise, that he's just another courtly, charming Southern man whose notion of appropriate physical distance is somewhat narrower than my own—a nice man who doesn't really like women (the ladies, God bless 'em).

I'm at ease with most of these men, though, even when they compare handiwork, after a presentation by one of the plastic surgeons, and the guys who are most pleased with their mastectomies begin lifting their shirts. It's like being in a room full of cardiac surgery survivors; everyone is telling stories, wagging fingers, showing what his doctor did for him. I see the scars from a distance, but it seems that the men wouldn't mind if I got closer. I take my cue from Aaron, a transsexual man in his late forties, enough like Joe Pesci to be his shorter, Southern brother. Aaron is taking photographs for his newsletter for ReCast, a nonprofit organization that provides information, referrals, and support for FTM transsexuals, and he is acting as my guide. When I am speechless, he acts as my interpreter.

One guy whose chest Aaron and I study looks like a blond sailor from the cover of a 1946 *Life* magazine. "It takes about three years for the body to settle down," this guy says, and as he rolls up his T-shirt to show the incision lines, tan and thickly ridged against his muscular torso, another man, middle-aged and narrow-chested, moves his tie and shyly opens his white shirt and shows me the incision marks around his nipples. I see, as I have never properly noticed, that the male chest, from nipple to collarbone, is configured completely differently from the female.

I'm cold, but Aaron unbuttons his cuffs. "Look around you," he says. All the guys have loosened their ties and rolled up their shirtsleeves. "Testosterone heats up the system. We're all comfortable, but you're gonna freeze your butt off."

After the conference, Aaron provides introductions to some wives and significant others. The first one I talk to is Aaron's girlfriend.

Samantha, forty-two, met Aaron through a personal ad. "I had dated women, and I had a bad dating experience with a genetic man, so I was looking at the personals: gay, straight, and alternative. And this was *alternative*. I didn't have to go through the anguish of his transition—I just met this man. And although I wasn't attracted to him physically right away, I was very attracted to his energy and his vigor. That testosterone, it's really something.

"I thought it would be very different from being with a genetic man, but it turns out to be not so different after all. There's nothing female about him. Sometimes I wish there was . . . just a little more female style in him. I said to my friend Mitzi that men are all wrapped up with their cocks, whether they have them or not. It's still all testosterone and power and having balls, one way or another."

Bridget is the journalist who became James Green's girlfriend.

"I thought, as a feminist, This is horrible—these are crazy women, self-hating women who find these unscrupulous, misogynistic surgeons to lop off their breasts. I had met a few of these guys, and I had read a few books by feminists on the subject. Transsexuals seemed pretty wacky.

"But after two hours with Jamie, I was very attracted, and I think I fell in love with him the next day. I went for a walk and began fantasizing about him sexually. I had asked him, for the article, to show me the surgery, and we were both embarrassed, we laughed, but he showed me. And my first, my spontaneous response to what I saw was, 'Oh, that's so cute!' And it was. I have friends—straight friends—who think I've given up something important because he doesn't have a regular penis. It wasn't a loss to me. We have a lot more variety. We make love to each other, after all, not to organs."

Her tone of fond reminiscence, the affection she holds not only for the lover but for the joy the lover has given, frays, and her voice tightens to a sharp New York buzz. "I saw him as a combination of female and male, and he was sane and he was a feminist . . . sort of. I thought, I'm tired of men, I'm tired of women, here's someone completely *new.* But now we're dealing with the same old man-woman thing, like with any other man. And we're struggling. Suddenly, I can totally relate to my friend who has been complaining about her husband for years.

"I'm convinced—I know otherwise, but I'm convinced—that he was never really a woman."

Lucy Davis, widowed after eighteen years of marriage and with two teenagers, thinks that meeting Forrest was her destiny. She saw Forrest's name on the patient roster at the hospital where she's a social worker, and the name struck her, although she couldn't imagine why. "I just knew that I would know this man. I finally met him two years later in a store. He flirted with me, I recognized his name, and I knew he was the one." After they dated for a while, he told her about his surgery. "He told me with his eyes closed, he couldn't look at me. And when he opened them, he said, 'You're still here?' And I said that it wasn't a problem. We've been together ever since 1982."

Forrest is an editor, and no one in New Hampshire, not his in-laws, not his stepchildren, certainly not his colleagues and neighbors or the guys on his softball team, knows. "We're pretty paranoid here in the closet," Lucy says. "Otherwise we're like all other heterosexual couples, up and down over the years. I can live with his body and his scars. He always says he has a cock, it's just a little bit smaller than other guys'. That testosterone, you know. I never had a lesbian relationship, and I still haven't had one. I like guys. I love this one."

Michael is the pseudonym he has asked me to use for him, and I cannot describe his comfortable home or the company he runs. He does not go to events like American Fantasia. His former therapist contacted him, and he agreed to talk with me on neutral ground, at a friend's apartment. We're meeting in the late morning, and I buy three sandwiches, a dozen cookies, and two kinds of soda at a fancy deli, but he doesn't eat. He is a serious, dark-skinned black man dressed in corporate casual for a Saturday with his relatives, whom he announces he plans to join before too long. I take him for thirty-eight or so, but he is ten years older than that. (I don't know if I have just never noticed that men usually look younger than women their age, or if it's something in the skin of these particular men—some vestige of former female smoothness—or if it's having had a second, hormonally powerful adolescence later in life, but all the transsexual men look to me at least five years younger than they are.) After two hours, Michael is less nervous than when we began, but he is never relaxed. About half an hour before he leaves, he takes a cookie and a sip of club soda.

"I grew up in a nice, materially comfortable middle-class

life. But. I carried a deep, dark secret around with me. I was pretty strange anyway. I was not an easy child to raise—my mother had her times with me. I believed that my feelings mattered, even though I was a child. I was an *offensive* child. I would not be taken advantage of, I would not be ordered about. I was just a short person, but a person. I know a kid just like that now. Completely obnoxious. I love him.

"I hate to sound like Marlo Thomas, but I just wanted to be free to be me, whatever that was. And I didn't know, although I kept going to the library, trying to find out. Until I was six, I was a happy child. Boy games, boy clothes, even a little girlfriend up the street. And after going off to school, horrified that I had to go in what felt like drag, sure that everyone would laugh at me, I knew that I'd better get used to it, because this body was not becoming male and it clearly made a difference to the world. I tried to do what I was supposed to in adolescence, tried to be the Last Lady, like my mother and my sisters, which I did pretty well. I didn't even bother trying to be a tomboy, it would have been absurd by then. My breasts were huge—they were ridiculous, size 46 double Z. But Joan of Arc did it for me, explained me to me, when I encountered her in school at the age of nine. I thought, Well, here we go, and when I was twelve, finally, I found a book on transsexuals.

"After graduate school," Michael continues, shaking his head over another five wasted years, "I thought, Well, maybe I'm a lesbian. Could be—I know I'm attracted to women. I went to consciousness-raising meetings, and I'd listen and feel like a fraud. One girl said, 'What makes each of us feel like a real woman?' and while they went around the room answering, I thought, Nothing. Absolutely nothing on earth makes me feel like a woman.

"I'm just a plain old heterosexual man, and I didn't want to spend my life having relationships with women who had never, ever been with a woman before and didn't know why they were attracted to me. I wanted a life. I'm not a professional transsexual. I don't think of myself as transsexual anymore. I was one, I made that transition, now I'm just a man."

Michael says, "Let me tell you about my terminally polite family." And although he himself borders on the terminally polite, he tells me funny, sad, outrageous family stories, the kind we all use to entertain company, deflect sympathy, and connect without too much feeling. His father, born early enough in this century to have heard stories of slavery from *his* father, always told Michael that he was entitled to be happy, and that God would not have put such an unusual child on this earth without purpose.

"He said to me, 'You're not the first freak in the family, and you're not likely to be the last.' My poor mother. I'm dead to her. We see each other, we love each other, but the loss of her daughter was terrible. And I feel her pain. But I couldn't do otherwise. I know she would have preferred the husband, the kids, the house, and the Valium, but I couldn't. The first time someone suggested I might want to kiss a man, I thought, Don't be ridiculous."

At funerals and weddings, the old folks who had known Michael before puberty as a tough little girl nicknamed Butch were comfortable with him. And the young kids would call him over to their table at the party and brag to their friends, "Go on, Uncle Mike. Tell them how you used to be a girl. Tell them." One elderly uncle approached him at a funeral. "So, you're a man now. Well, well. How you doin'? How's your health?" And when Michael said that his health was fine, thank you, the old man sat him down for twenty minutes so they could talk about his rheumatism.

"They figured I had my health, I had a job, God bless me. My aunt figured my mother needed a strong man to lean on, so God sent me. Indirectly, of course. I keep my blinders on, they serve me. I kept not receiving family wedding invitations, and I was so dense I'd call and say, 'Where's my invitation?' And since in my terminally polite family there's no way you could tell someone they weren't invited, I kept showing up. After I found myself seated with the unemployed third cousin and his trashy girlfriend, I knew I wasn't wanted and I kept thinking, 'Why didn't they say so?' But they couldn't say so, and I finally figured it out."

"And did you keep going anyway?"

"Hell, no." He sits back and opens his tight hands. He makes himself smile, and his dimples show. "I was born black. I don't expect people to like me, to accept me. Some transsexuals, especially the white MTFs, they're in shock after the transition. Loss of privilege, loss of status—they think people should be thrilled to work side by side with them. Well, people do not go to work in mainstream America hoping for an educational experience. I didn't expect anyone to be happy to see me—I just expected, I demanded, a little tolerance. Hell, I transitioned on the job. I didn't even tell people what was going on. You remember I said I was an offensive *child*? A friend of mine said, 'Uh, don't you think you ought to say something? People want to know.' And I said, 'Let 'em ask.' The transition was hard, but once I was completely male, people relaxed.

"I'm the same personality—a little more visually responsive erotically, maybe a little more aggressive, but I was always aggressive. You know what's different? I have a toolbox. My whole life, I never thought about one, I'm not a big fixer. But now, every once in a while, I find myself buying another wrench, or one of those very small screwdrivers. That's different.

"I'm prepared to make my own way. And I am. I've been fortunate—I've been loved, I've been married, I'm not an addict, not unemployed, not dysfunctional. I'm a decent person, I'm not ashamed. I don't know why this condition chose me. We, people who have been through this transition—we are among the few people in the world who have overcome obstacles and fulfilled their lifelong dreams. All these obstacles, and I am who I dreamed I'd be, who I wanted to be. I'll marry again, I'm going ahead with an adoption as a single man, my work's going well. I'm damned fortunate."

CONSERVATIVE MEN IN CONSERVATIVE DRESSES

HETEROSEXUAL CROSSDRESSERS

Heterosexual crossdressers bother almost everyone. Gay people regard them with disdain or affectionate incomprehension, something warmer than tolerance, but not much. Transsexuals regard them as men "settling" for crossdressing because they don't have the courage to act on their transsexual longing, or else as closeted gay men so homophobic that they prefer wearing a dress to facing their desire for another man. Other straight men tend to find them funny or sad, and some find them enraging. The only people on whose kindness and sympathy crossdressers can rely are women: their wives, and even more dependably, their hairdressers, their salespeople, their photographers and makeup artists, their electrolysists, their therapists, and their friends.

Drag queens (gay crossdressers) make sense to most of us. There is a congruence of sexual orientation, appearance, and temperament: feminine gay men dressing as women for a career, like RuPaul, or less lucratively, as prostitutes, or to express their own sense of theater and femininity. (Barney Frank as a drag queen makes no more sense, intuitively, than Dick Cheney.) Actors whose most famous performance is as a female, like Barry Humphries's brilliant and textured Dame Edna or Flip Wilson's one-note gag of Geraldine, don't puzzle us. Tootsie and Mrs. Doubtfire and the boys in *Some Like It Hot* don't puzzle us; they're just men doing what they have to do to survive, learning a nice lesson about the travails of womanhood and giving one on the benign uses of masculine self-esteem. Even the crossdressing women of history, from Pope Joan to Joan of Arc to America's jazz-playing Billy Tipton, from Little Jo Monaghan the cowpoke to Disney's adorable Mulan, don't puzzle us; they chose to live as men because they couldn't otherwise have the lives they wanted.

Every fall, hundreds of heterosexual crossdressers come to Provincetown for Fantasia Fair, an annual event since 1975. They come to attend seminars on self-esteem and lectures on Your Feminine Self, to accompany their wives to support group meetings, and to pay for photo sessions of themselves "en femme." They come to walk up and down Commercial Street, to eat in the Governor Bradford and Fat Jack's, simply to be and be seen in public dressed as women. Provincetown seems like a pretty safe place for them, and it is, but even here there are looks and chuckles, and there is no sign that any of the residents, gay or straight, recognize these men as people with whom they have much in common. The gay people do not say, "Oh, you're a straight man who likes to wear a dress? Welcome aboard!" And the straight men do not say, "Well, except for the dress thing, you're just like me. Howdy, pardner!"

Heterosexual crossdressers—straight men who have not only a wish but a need to wear women's clothes and accessories—manage to be marginal among heterosexual men, marginal among other men who wear women's clothes, marginal in the community of sexual minorities, and completely acceptable only to fetishists, who accept anyone who says they belong.

Many heterosexual crossdressers never come out of the closet, not even to their wives; they spend their whole adult lives dressing in secret, ordering size 20 cocktail dresses from catalogues, with only the mirror for company. Others tell their wives after ten or twenty or thirty years of marriage, sometimes because they've been caught wearing her clothes, sometimes because the clothes have been discovered. (The revelation that he himself is the "other woman" is a staple of crossdresser histories, and although the husbands say that their wives were relieved, it's not clear to me that they were, for more than a minute.) Second wives usually get told sooner, and as with other matters, third wives tend to know everything there is to know before the knot is tied.

But a lot of these men want to crossdress outside their bedrooms, driven by loneliness, by unmet narcissistic needs (all dressed up and nowhere to go), by risk-taking impulses (it's not hard to grasp that a forty-five-year-old, two-hundred-forty-pound former Marine strolling through the Mall of America in full drag is consciously courting risk). They go to get-togethers in Kansas City, in Pittsburgh, in Seattle, all over America. They make forays into malls in pairs, and they go to tolerant gay bars in small groups. They browse in the Belladona Plus Size Shop of Beverly, Massachusetts, and they hang out at the Criss/Cross Condo in Houston, which offers the Empress, Princess, and Duchess packages for a twenty-four-hour getaway as a woman. They go to weekly or monthly meetings, of six or ten or twenty guys, at the Paradise Club in Parma, Ohio, at Long Island Femme Expression in Ozone Park, at gatherings of the Central Florida Sisters of Kissimmee. There are crossdresser groups in Nashua, New Hampshire, and Trenton, New Jersey, in Springfield, Missouri, and Allentown, Pennsylvania, and throughout the Bible Belt. There are enough crossdressers in Arizona to support chapters in Phoenix and Tucson. A man who crossdresses and needs to be seen crossdressed can go to conferences like Provincetown's Fantasia Fair or Atlanta's Southern Comfort or the Midwest's Fall Harvest, or take a cruise aboard the *Holiday,* a Carnival ship offering a four-day trip to Catalina out of Los Angeles, happily hosting twenty-five crossdressers and their spouses amidst the other thousand guests.

Sometimes the wives wish to come, to support their husbands and enjoy the trip, or to hang out with other wives, like golf widows or wives in Al-Anon. Some come because their husbands need them to. "I don't mind, but really, if he could learn to do his makeup properly and fasten his own bra, I'd rather stay home," one woman told me at Fall Harvest 2000, in St. Louis. (Later she called to say that she had bought her husband a home video guide to makeup for men and a magnifying mirror, and that she was resigning as his dresser. "He can ask one of the other guys to hook his bra.") Happy wives are everyone's favorites, but happy or cowed, enthusiastic or grimly accepting, the wives at all of these functions are simultaneously important objects of much public appreciation and utterly secondary to the men's business. The world of crossdressers is for the most part a world of traditional men, traditional marriages, and truths turned inside out.

I am on line to board the *Holiday* and my antennae are up. So far, I have seen three large families, one Filipino, one African American, one mixed Caucasian and African American. There are lots of couples in their twenties, some with six suitcases, some with small gym bags. There are several pairs of well-dressed women who are clearly travel agents. I keep scanning the crowd for the crossdressers, but no one stands out.

As I make my way to my small room on B Deck, I wonder what to wear to dinner and a preliminary cocktail party in the suite of my hosts, Mel and Peggy Rudd, both blond, heavyset Texans in their sixties. Peggy has written a number of books on crossdressing, the best known of which is *My Husband Wears My Clothes* (PM Publishers), and was formerly the director of SPICE (Spouses' and Partners' International Conference for Education), an annual workshop that "focuses on spouses' and partners' issues, communication skills and relationship-building" for wives of "ordinary heterosexual men with an additional feminine dimension." I've met the Rudds before. I've traveled to Texas to interview them, stayed at their home, woken up in their astonishingly sunny and beribboned guest room, and walked down to the breakfast nook past a phalanx of posed photos: the Rudds with Ronald Reagan, the Rudds with both Reagans, the Rudds with George and Barbara Bush. At breakfast, Peggy said to Mel,

"Oh dear, we should have taken down all those pictures of us with famous Republicans before Amy got here." Mel smiled. "Oh, I think she's a true liberal, she won't mind about the Republicans."

I waffle about what to wear for nearly half an hour. Outside my door, the men are coming down the hall in twos and threes. Finally I decide that silk pants and a tank top and sandals is right—right for the level of dressiness of the dinner (which I have overestimated) and right for my own social and appearance anxiety (which I have underestimated). When I walk into the little party, the Rudds hug me and introduce me to everyone as "Amy the writer." Some men flinch, although the Rudds have told everyone to expect me. Tory, a good-looking young man from Mexico, shakes my hand: "Hello, Miss Amy." His aunt and his cousin and his girlfriend, Cory, are on this trip, his first time crossdressing in public. Tory and Cory, with their romantic banter, his devoted relatives, and his final painstaking and successful transformation from Antonio Banderas to Daisy Fuentes, become the darlings of our group; they make everyone feel better.

I meet the rest of the guys and their wives. The men—to whom I will refer in print as "he," and to whom I refer in person when they are crossdressed as "she"—are not drag queens, hardworking perennials like Pearlene the Size Queen and Big-Boned Barbie, not actors, not Vegas female impersonators. They are most definitely not gender-benders of any kind, not Marilyn Manson, not Prince. They are more like Mrs. Attanas, my formidable fourth-grade teacher, a big, tall lady with a bolsterlike bosom, thick legs, sensible pumps, hennaed hair, and twin spots of rouge on her cheeks. I meet a happy, long-married couple, Steve and Sue, who look alike whether he's crossdressed or not. I meet Harry, who is always somewhat crossdressed (women's jeans, women's sneakers) but never flamboyantly; his appearance is that of an effeminate man, and he doesn't bother with a femme name or seem to have any of the common need for a more feminine presentation and feminine affectations. I would have thought that this might be easier for his wife than a husband who calls himself Lulu, spends hours in the bathroom on his face, and parades around the living room in a strapless lavender tulle dress and matching fuck-me pumps, but it's not.

"I love him," she tells me later. "I love him, but I don't want a man who is excited by the idea of being a woman. We have two kids, he's a great dad, a good provider, but I want a man who's comfortable with masculinity. I don't want to be sisters . . . or lesbians. If I wanted a woman, I would have found one by now. But . . . there's all the other things that are good." And he tells me later, with great sadness, "She is the most supportive person in the world, and this is a terrible thing for her. We work on it, we struggle." He stops and gathers his defenses; throughout the cruise he will condescend to the men with femme names, the men who insist on hours of makeup, because he sees himself as "evolved," free of the trappings and compulsions of crossdressing. "All couples struggle, they fight about money, about sex. You can't tell me they don't. This is no different." He looks out at the ocean. "This is different, I know, but I refuse to let it ruin our lives."

At dinner I am seated at a table anchored by Peggy and

Melanie (as Mel calls himself when en femme), in nearly matching vibrant floral prints. To my right are Tory's aunt and cousin, who speak almost no English, and next to them is a very attractive woman, Lori, a Lee Remick look-alike, husband nowhere in sight. To my left are Felicity and his wife. Felicity is a large, hunched man, made up in a conventional, slightly stiff manner. He looks like a librarian, or perhaps the strong-minded wife of a minister, and he is, in the rest of the world, a Southern Baptist minister from the very buckle of the Bible Belt.

"So, you're the writer. Well, I'd say you pass pretty well," Felicity tells me. I smile pleasantly, as if I am not offended, as if I didn't think he intended to offend me. "Well," he says heartily, and then he clears his throat twice and stares at my silk pants. "You gals just get to crossdress all the time and no one says boo." He sounds furious that life is so easy for me and so hard for him, but because he is a minister, and even more because he is dressed as and representing someone named Felicity, he cannot be direct or angry; he has to try to convey a serene and gracious femininity regardless of his feelings and the oddness of the setting, which is as hard for him to do as it would be for me. And his wife is beside herself, tight-lipped, hands clasped; she is a Christian woman doing what she must, and as much as she might wish it otherwise, what she cannot be is pleased.

On the other side of me is a man in his late sixties, recently retired as a senior partner in a white-shoe law firm in the Deep South. He looks great. He looks like a Neiman Marcus matron, right down to his Chanel slingbacks, and although he seems a bit out of place, it is only because the cruise is so downscale and there are twenty-year-old guys clumping around the casino in their NASCAR jackets, baseball caps, and hiking boots, as if a nice shirt and a pair of slacks would be way too much trouble.

At first I thought that the matronly look so common to straight crossdressers reflected some weird attachment to the mother, that the image they wished to present was that of their own first woman—hence the heavy foundation, the blue eyeshadow, the big pearl button earrings. I no longer think so. That same look is common among their wives, and among lots of middle-aged women not much interested in changing fashions.

Most crossdressers, and almost all married crossdressers, live lives in which they are not crossdressed. They don't take female hormones, they usually don't have electrolysis even if they would like to (many express the wish to wake up and find themselves without facial, arm, or leg hair, but their wives are opposed), and they are not regular readers of *Elle, Vogue,* or even *Ladies' Home Journal.* They cannot easily put together a natural, believable female appearance. First, you need beard camouflage to flatten and disguise the stubble, then powder over that and foundation over that, and sweating is a big problem. (Jim Bridges, a transformation guide and guru, creator of the *Bridges to Beauty 2000* and *Hollywood Makeup Secrets* videos, which are offered at his boutique in California and through his booming Internet business—"Can't tell you who in the House of Representatives, can't tell you who in the NFL," he says to me while putting false eyelashes on a John Deere salesman at Fall Harvest—counsels a quick swipe of antiperspirant on the upper lip and at the hairline. Crossdressing is not only anxiety-provoking and arousing, it is also warm under the wig, the corset, the padding, the pantyhose.) You need the foundation for smoothness and for color, and by the time you add lipstick and a wig, if you're a man you get that overdone crossdresser look and if you're a woman you get Joan Collins. A pronounced face requires pronounced makeup for balance, and after the false eyelashes and even the most subtle contouring of the wider jaw, the thick brow, one can look beautiful or ridiculous, but one cannot look like most of the women around.

My tablemates look like more attractive versions of the photos I've seen in the personals sections at the back of crossdresser magazines. I flipped through thirty issues of *Transgender Tapestry* and saw a lot of men who looked bad, like every joke and caricature of a crossdresser: the big shoulders, the jagged makeup, the prom dresses or JCPenney crushed-velvet tube dresses. Some looked mentally ill and possibly dangerous. I saw a few beautiful women, very often transsexual, as it turned out, but occasionally just crossdressers blessed with the right shape and the conventional proportions, narrow shoulders, small hands. And then there were always a dozen crossdressers who looked like pleasant, average women: librarians, day-care providers, schoolteachers, not staggering, not intense, not lovely, but perfectly ordinary, pantsuited, sensibly shod middle-aged women. I have met crossdressers whose presentation is just this side of Christina Aguilera, and I have met a fifty-year-old Midwestern engineer and a sixty-year-old born-again Christian CEO and a forty-year-old police captain, all of whom dress exactly as they would if they had been born to the distaff side, in clothes both contemporary and appropriate, whether Gap or Escada or Dress Barn. Anatomy may not be destiny, but it certainly lays a hand on our options.

Age is a great help to crossdressers. It is, for us all, the great androgynizer; the skin softens and sags, the secondary sex characteristics shrink and fade, slacken and thin. I have seen far more convincing crossdressers over sixty than under. Except for the guys whose height and build make it impossible for the world to construe them as female (and this is a problem for very tall and muscular women, as well), by sixty, crossdressing men have undergone the inevitable softening of the face and chest, the diminution of testosterone, and have enough practice and enough confidence to make very passable grandmothers of themselves. Not surprisingly, the amount of time that many crossdressers spend en femme triples after they retire. They can crossdress when they want, and many of them want to a lot.

There are twenty-five crossdressers among the four hundred or so male passengers aboard the *Holiday,* and this may represent roughly their proportion of the general population, but it's impossible to say for sure. No one seems to have any reliable statistics about how many heterosexual crossdressers there are. I check with the International Foundation for Gender Education in Waltham, Massachusetts, which acts as switchboard, referral service, news agency, and educational center for both crossdressers and transsexuals, and with GenderPAC (Gender Public Advocacy Coalition), and with Dallas Denny of AEGIS (American Educational Gender Information Service), a longtime activist in the transsexual community, but none of them can tell me. "Too many guys in the closet," a voice at the IFGE says. "How could anyone presume to count?"

I call Ray Blanchard, a self-described "traditional clinician," who is head of clinical sexology services at Canada's Centre for Addiction and Mental Health and has been studying sexuality for thirty years. "No one knows," he says. "I consulted several colleagues, and the consensus is that there's no useful epidemiological information. Period."

I check with Jane Ellen and Mary Frances Fairfax of Tri-Ess, the Society for the Second Self, "a family-oriented support group for heterosexual crossdressers." The Fairfaxes (this is the last name they use for their crossdressing life, their mutual invented femme name) live in Texas, where Jane Ellen is otherwise Chet, and a physician, and a fierce cribbage player and the father of three boys, two in college, one in prep school. They offer that at last count there were eleven hundred crossdressers and three hundred twenty wives in Tri-Ess's thirty chapters nationwide, but they don't know how many heterosexual crossdressers there are either.

"Maybe three or four million," Jane Ellen hazards. "Maybe somewhere between three and five percent of the population. People who claim it's more, I think that's just, you know, a minority wanting to be bigger than it is. And people who say more like one or two percent, I think those are the ones who are ashamed." When I ask Ray Blanchard for an estimate, he says he thinks three to five percent of the population is about right too.

These are just about the only two points of agreement between Blanchard and the Fairfaxes: no one knows how many heterosexual crossdressers there are, and all these men in dresses who assert that they are straight, sometimes to the point of annoying everyone else, are straight. They may not be straight in exactly the way that noncrossdressing men are—most heterosexual men don't look at an attractive woman and think, I'd like to have sex with her, I'd like to wear her dress, I'd like men and women to look at me as they look at her—but they are straight.

It was precisely for these men that Tri-Ess was founded in 1976, as a melding of several crossdressing groups, including the historic Hose and Heels Club, which began meeting in California in 1961, and is to many crossdressers what Stonewall is to gay men: the beginning of the end of shame (although not, for the crossdressers, the end of fiercely preserved anonymity). Tri-Ess is now the largest organization for heterosexual crossdressers and their spouses, by which they mean wives, and although nobody would object if a female-to-male crossdresser and her husband wanted to join, it is true that they have not yet, and it is true that neither the folks at Tri-Ess nor I can quite imagine the dynamics of that couple, since the spousal role requires an abundance of traditional wifely virtues: accommodation, compromise, and gracious acceptance of that which is unwelcome, and often truly painful.

The "spouses and partners" who are mentioned so frequently in Tri-Ess literature and who attend the SPICE workshop, which Tri-Ess sponsors, are women.

The Fairfaxes, a little John Gray, a little country doctor in their beaming certainty and parental concern for the weaknesses of others, are the driving forces behind Tri-Ess. For some crossdressers, Tri-Ess is a beacon of hope in a society that judges them weirdos and queers when they know they are not. For critics within the crossdressing community, the Fairfaxes are good people, but misguided about the nature of crossdressing, even self-deceiving. Lots of crossdressers take issue with the Tri-Ess focus on "family values" and heterosexuality. The Tennessee Vals, for instance, will welcome you "if you consider yourself a crossdresser, transsexual or any other type of gender bender . . . whether gay or straight, bisexual or asexual." There is a big-tent movement among crossdressers these days, and many groups don't share Tri-Ess's exclusionary philosophy.

Jane Ellen Fairfax is a man with a mission: to save crossdressers from their worst selves and to save their marriages. Mary Frances, firm but unassuming, competent, and mild except when offended, is his partner in this, and has been the secretary of Tri-Ess's board of directors (of which Jane Ellen is the chair) since 1988.

Jane Ellen has a hearty, blunt demeanor that is sugared over in the Southern manner when he's crossdressed, more emphatic when he's "en drab," as they say, but he is always smart, always tenacious and unshakable in his self-esteem and in his beliefs, which include churchgoing Christianity and the platform of the Republican party. He sees crossdressing as more than a hobby and something quite different from a problem. He insists that the wearing of women's clothes is both relaxing and expressive of a feminine self that is nurturing and gentle, and that can enhance any marriage if the wife is wise enough to appreciate it and strong enough to corral what can be, as Jane Ellen admits, a narcissistic, self-indulgent habit.

Once a wife or partner realizes her mate isn't leaving her for another man or for a new life as a woman, or taking risks that could destroy their financial and family life, the two of them can seek a balanced solution. . . . Many of the traits that attracted her in the first place—sensitivity, kindness, appreciation of beauty, etc.—can now be seen as belonging to that "woman within."

[Tri-Ess pamphlet, "Do You Know Someone Who Is a Cross Dresser?" February 2000]

A central tenet of Tri-Ess is that crossdressing is a gift.

Crossdressers are blessed with an additional facet to our personalities. As we accept our dual, masculine-and-feminine, "bi-gendered" gift, and seek to understand and explore it, the result is a very fulfilling broadening of our entire personality. . . . Our occasional adoption of a complete feminine persona and total gender role presentation is an outward personal expression of our inner feminine feelings. We dress appropriately in emulation, rather than in mockery, of femi-

ninity. . . . We cultivate our complete feminine image, with lingerie, makeup, wig, padding for breasts and hips, as well as feminine clothing, shoes and accessories and even a femme name.

[Tri-Ess pamphlet, "Tri-Ess Today," 2000]

The Fairfaxes hope to persuade the world outside Tri-Ess that heterosexual crossdressers are just normal folks, not at all like those gender outlaws and gender-benders—bearded men in dresses, "chicks with dicks"—whom Jane Ellen calls "gender mockers." The Fairfaxes want crossdressers out of the closet, not because Tri-Ess wishes to defy or upend society, but because they believe that if society understood how normal crossdressing is, there would be no resistance to it; it would be seen as no stranger a form of relaxation than golf. The words that Ray Blanchard uses when he talks about crossdressing—"fetish," "continuum of gender dysphoria," "erotic self-absorption"—are words the Fairfaxes don't ever want to hear. It upsets them to have crossdressing viewed as being about sex, which they try to get as far away from as possible, or as odd, although they know it is, because they also know that they are exactly the kind of people—Christians, family people, Texans—that George W. Bush wants and needs. When you say "crossdresser," Jane Ellen and Mary Frances want you to think only of a guy relaxing in a dress.

"Of course it's not relaxing," Blanchard says, with some heat. "Heels and makeup and a wig and a corset? It's preposterous. Even women don't find that relaxing. Relaxing is a pair of sweatpants, clothing that doesn't even feel like clothing. Crossdressers want to normalize this, to have it seen as relaxation and self-expression. I've had people say to me, 'You know, I bet if there wasn't all this stereotyping, these people would not choose to wear a dress.' I say that's nonsense. The crossdressing is an attempt to resolve an internal conflict, and it's not about fabric. If we had clothing that was identical in every way, including fabric and shape, except men wore shirts with four buttons and women had shirts with five, crossdressers would want more than anything to have the shirt with five. We don't know why."

Our categories and our descriptions are so narrow and self-protective that not only don't we have words for the drive to crossdress, we don't have any language to describe the mixture of attraction and envy that often leads these men to have sex with women while thinking of themselves as male lesbians, "men trapped in men's bodies," in Dr. Anne Lawrence's words. For crossdressers, Ray Blanchard says, "it's like they plug in the lamp and the toaster pops up. They emulate the women they want to have—some kind of confusion between attraction to a sexual object and being the object. Many see an attractive woman, get aroused and then envious. They cannot get their wires uncrossed."

A brochure from the Fantasia Fair of 1986 encapsulates the crossdressers' bind.

What is a Crossdresser?

An individual, usually heterosexual, who desires and needs to dress in the clothing of the opposite sex at different times throughout his or her life. This compulsive behavior generally starts at a young age and the individual struggles alone for many years with this closeted need. Cross-Dressing is not a sickness, but represents a person who enjoys expressing another aspect of his personality and gains both emotional and physical pleasure from this transition. It is not a hobby, but a necessity and Cross-dressing is for life.

This seems to me to be the heart of the crossdressers' dilemma, and now the heart of mine in writing about them. Crossdressing is a compulsion, but somehow not a sickness. A good wife should tolerate it because the man has no choice, but it shouldn't be too hard to tolerate because it is, after all, a gift. It is about enjoyment, it gives physical and emotional pleasure—and it's a necessity. The necessity of crossdressing is frightening to the men and to their wives, and their wish to tame it, to dress it up as a preference and a superior personality, is understandable.

"We learn what everyone learns," Jane Ellen Fairfax says. "Girls are now taught you can be anything you want to be. No one tells a little boy, 'You can be a sweet, soft, and wonderful little boy and an astronaut.' Men are still being trained—well, you know, as Virginia Prince [founder of Tri-Ess and one of the godmothers of crossdressing] says, 'Men are always trying to become what women are content to be.' "

"What is it that women are content to be?" I ask.

"Oh, you know, they know when to give it a rest. They know when and how to quit. They can relax and be themselves."

I do know. He means that in his vision, idealized and old-fashioned, women are like oceans, or like fields, or like horses, and men are sailors, farmers, and cowboys, and that is their curse and that is women's blessing, although women may not realize it. It is exhausting to be a man, and delightful to kick off those demands and slip into something more comfortable. It no longer seems odd to me, when I am talking to the Fairfaxes, that they are middle-of-the-road Republicans; it seems odd only that this quirk, this habit of wearing women's clothing, would make anyone think that they belonged at the same party as Queer Nation, Dykes on Bikes, and transsexual women who become lesbian feminists.

Jane Ellen says, "Crossdressers are not women, and they're not trying to be women." When he talks about crossdressers, he almost always says "they." When he talks about his marriage, his practice, and his politics, he says "I."

"A lot of men want to go there, to be our feminine selves, to slow down and stop striving."

"It sounds like yoga," I say.

Jane Ellen is silent. It sounds like yoga except for the two hours of preparation time. It sounds like yoga except that it begins in a man's life as an erotic response and becomes an erotic fetish. Sometimes I put on lipstick when I'm tense. It makes me feel armored, less vulnerable to the world. That's not the same thing. I don't feel that the lipstick is essential to my being, that without it I must stay home, and even as I know that there is an erotic dimension to getting dressed up (it's not just crossdressers who appreciate the rustle of a slip, the slide of a stocking), when the dressing and the garments are the fuel and the expression of one's sexual wishes, it is about sex, and not gender. For all their talk of relaxation, the Fairfaxes are too smart to think, or to try to persuade me, that crossdressing is ordinary, or that it's just a hobby. Fly-fishing is a hobby; spending two hours preparing yourself to walk through a mall or a hotel lobby, hoping—hoping to the point of anxiety and arousal—that you will be perceived as female, is not what anyone, not least the crossdressers themselves, thinks of as a hobby.

"Crossdressers' desires do not map onto anything in our world," Ray Blanchard says. "You will never know how they feel if you are not one of them. And they have to disconnect between reality and their fantasy. Otherwise, it's too disruptive. It's too disruptive to acknowledge that you wish your penis was part of your wife's body and not yours. It's too disruptive to acknowledge that this is a sexual compulsion—one that diminishes over time, to the point that you can begin to tame it and not be so driven by the sex part, but there are very few former crossdressers. Even when the sexual spark, the libido fades, the attachment and the need persist. Like in marriage."

Heterosexual crossdressers are disproportionately represented among the retired military; they are often firstborn sons, and often quite masculine-looking, which is why the rest of us struggle so with their appearance. Blanchard says, "All of these men will tell you, 'I had to hide my femininity. I became a cop, a firefighter, a black belt in karate, a construction worker, in order to compensate, in order to put these fears to rest and to hide my true nature.'" Blanchard thinks that what the men fear is actually exposure and ridicule—exposure not of their own femininity but of their drive to crossdress. He thinks their insistence that their intensely masculine behavior is merely a screen for their deeply feminine natures helps them believe that their wearing of women's clothes expresses this femininity rather than an erotic compulsion. "These are masculine guys, for the most part. There's no contradiction between 'I feel like a woman' and 'I drive a tank, fly combat, play tight end,' but there is a contradiction between those activities and 'I am a very feminine person and always have been.' The past gets rewritten because of their enormous emotional need to believe in their own femininity as the source of the need to crossdress."

This is the only world I know where heterosexual men argue that they are more feminine than they appear and their critics and judges argue that they are less.

It is Talent Night aboard the *Holiday,* and I am having dinner at the Rudds' table before the show. Felicity and Merrie, a large, sweet engineering professor, take turns dominating the dinner conversation. There is a great deal that they both want me to understand, and they are also gratified, painfully gratified, by my attention, by the fact that I even think about them without horror. I come to see why so many women find themselves sympathetic to crossdressers: women are raised to be sympathetic, and protective toward the vulnerable, and there is something appealing, unexpected, and powerful about being a woman and sympathizing with a man not because he demands it and you must offer it but because you genuinely feel sorry for him, for his debilitating envy and his anxious and powerless state of mind. Heidi Klum and her supermodel crowd may feel sorry for helpless men, whipsawed by passion, every night of the week, but this is not a stance that society affords most women.

Peggy Rudd is the boss and the model for the wives, their spokesperson, the movement's spokesperson, the cruise director, the school nurse. Mel, all hearty kindness, a genial grandfather even in a dress and bolero jacket, does not seem to have the same obligation. None of the men say to me, "I've learned so much from Mel." Like many husbands of dynamic, take-charge women, he is one of Peggy's biggest fans, supportive and teasing, emphatically appreciative, and just slightly digging in his heels. "She's just go, go, go," he says. He is a good old boy in drag, always looking for a laugh, a little good-natured fun, another party, another piece of bread and butter under Peggy's watchful eye (the whole table knows of his cholesterol troubles and hers). Although he does not make a pretty woman, he makes a reasonably good overweight, coarse-featured sixty-year-old woman, I think, but my eyes have adjusted: none of these guys look as tall or as large to me as they are.

With a slightly pursed expression, Peggy says, "My next book is on joy. The difference between the level of joy that crossdressers experience"—she holds her hand up over her head—"and the level of joy that their wives experience." Her hand drops to her waist. The crossdressers around us say nothing. They nod, joyous astronauts sympathizing with the poor wives left behind and trying not to show how much more fun they're having. I think of the twinkle in Mel's eyes and the fact that there is never anything like a twinkle in Peggy's. It must be psychologically exhausting for her to turn this pain into a shared hobby, his compulsion into entertainment, his need into an occasion for celebration, and I feel ashamed that knowing all that, I still prefer his company.

Peggy turns to Lori. "You are so special," she says, as she does every night. "You are just the most beautiful crossdresser I've ever seen. Everyone wants to sit next to you, you're so beautiful."

As I've learned in the past couple of days, Lori is a preoperative male-to-female transsexual; if she weren't with our group, she would stand out only as an unusually elegant woman on a Carnival cruise. Transsexuals sometimes come to transgender events, for a number of reasons, personal and political, but many feel that having resolved their problems through surgery, they have no need for the transgender community, for people who are defined as "other," and that they can now simply slip into the rest of America with legally changed ID and, like transgendered Anatole Broyards, enter into new lives and answer easier questions. Lori is here because she is accompanying one of her best friends, a crossdresser whose wife couldn't make it at the last minute.

The implication of Peggy's flattery is clear: your performance as a woman is so good. I don't think Peggy means to offend; she can't help it. Transsexuals make crossdressers nervous: maybe there is a continuum, maybe crossdressers just feel more mildly what transsexuals feel so deeply, and maybe those feelings will become overpowering if not reined in by wives and children and Tri-Ess's marital guidelines. Almost every crossdresser in the group compliments Lori. No wife has the nerve, or the wish, except Peggy. Other passengers send over requests for photographs with the beautiful crossdresser every night.

And Lori is deeply offended every night. If this were *Tootsie 2,* she would leap up, etiquette be damned, and say, "How dare you decide that I am the evening's entertainment? I don't ask the Don Rickles look-alike at Table Six to pose for us with his outrageous, hedgehoglike toupee. I don't send the waiter over to ask that the entire clan, three generations of short, pointy-headed, potbellied men, waddle over so I can show my friends the perils—not that I'm making a judgment—of inbreeding." And the entire dining room would cheer as Lori tossed her head prettily. If necessary, she would deck someone (although she doesn't have the build for it), which would be hilarious, and if the screenwriter had seen *In and Out,* all the waiters would don wigs and sing "I'm Every Woman" in their Thai, Mexican, South African, and Jamaican accents, until the insensitive slunk away or—as Peggy Rudd told me had happened on a previous cruise—the other guests began donning wigs too, partying along with and expressing envy for the fun-loving crossdressers.

This is not what happens. Lori withdraws, fending off the curious and the compliments, until she is as cool and pleasant as a white-gloved lady on the subway.

After dinner we make our way to the ship's theater for the talent show. It is an amazing evening, beginning with the small man who approaches us from behind potted plants leering like Groucho, murmuring "You ladies look lovely tonight" with the hopeful fatuity of John Cleese. The cross-dressers in our group dimple and smile, as if behind fans. "Aren't you nice?" one says. "Oh, thank you," says another, and bats her eyelashes. Lori says, "Give me a break," and walks into the theater. I follow, and bump into our group's shy, skinny engineer from Texas, from whom I have not heard a murmur so far, and who is now wobbling across the room in a white stretch velvet dress and a platinum Tina Turner shag.

Lori and I settle down in a booth; it's clear to me that she would rather not sit with the rest of the group, which has settled in a large, dim cluster on the other side of the stage. We are joined by a tiny elderly couple from South Africa, on their twenty-fifth cruise. The Tina Turner engineer approaches with another crossdresser, whom I haven't met, and then, at the last minute, sensing the utter lack of welcome, they pull back and join the larger group. I feel bad. Lori sighs. The elderly couple peer at the strange person in the tight white dress, and then at us, curiously. They are reassured, I think, although later I hear that Lori and Merrie have taken up with them and that they are as pleased to meet crossdressers as they have been to enjoy the chocolate buffet at midnight, to fox-trot in the Tahiti Lounge, and to visit the uninspiring port of Catalina. They seem incapable of having a bad time.

The engineer's companion, in a tiny bright red dress with matching red satin pumps and black fishnet hose, comes back across the floor to us with a camera. He takes four or five photos of Lori and me and our little South African friends. As usual, we are supposed to be flattered: either Lori is so beautiful, or we make such a charming group, that a crossdresser we don't know wishes to commemorate the occasion. Lori and I think that the photographer wants to show his friends at home how "real" both of us and therefore all of them look (and neither of us is flattered by that) or to suggest that the cruise has been an easy blending of the crossdressers and everyone else. Finally, smiling broadly, he leaves, with photos of us from every angle.

The emcee is English and unhappy. He mocks us all relentlessly and indiscriminately. He is as disgusted by the round-the-clock feeders as he is by the well-behaved reunion families and the blameless honeymoon couples; strolling on the deck and in the lounges, he assails us with cries of "You're having such fun!" much as an unhappy lover might scream, "You're ruining my life!"

The talent show opens with two couples from Japan demonstrating the rumba. The alpha couple, firmly occupying center stage, are in their late sixties and have been studying dance for about five years, or so I guess; it appears they speak no English, and the emcee gives only their names, with the same honeyed enthusiasm he reserves for the smallest children, the disabled, and the old. The beta couple are in their seventies and have been studying the rumba for about five minutes. They sway and snap their fingers ceremoniously and essay a few simple steps upstage while the other couple go from the basic box step into a hand-to-hand double break and twin turns, all slowly, elegantly, and with enormous intensity. The dancers are stately and exotic in black tie and rustling taffeta dresses, and even though their performance seems to take hours, they are applauded wildly.

The rumba people are followed by an Israeli man who plays a homemade drum with his mouth, an accountant who sings "Heartbreak Hotel" badly but arouses the crowd's snickering only when he attempts to mime the Presley moves, and a lady in her seventies who sings "I Believe" and clutches the emcee's hand. He begins supportively, swinging her hand gently, smiling genially, but his true nature asserts itself, and by the end of her song, he is pumping her arm, grinning and flapping like Jerry Lewis.

The next guest is one of ours. I noticed Ted the first night, a small, dapper blond man in a tux, and wondered if the *Holiday* had Gentlemen Escorts like the fancy ships do. Unlike the other crossdressers, he comes to dinner every night in high, black-tie drag: exquisite bouffant wigs, perfect matte make-up, three-inch heels, and formfitting dresses that cling to his padded bust and bottom. His wife looks pleasant and sensibly dressed, except for the one night when he is in a tux and she is in one of his outfits. For one night, she too looks like a beautiful drag queen, and even so, our crowd is more interested in his artistry than in her.

Ted's performance, not surprisingly, is Marilyn Monroe doing "Diamonds Are a Girl's Best Friend." Ted asks the emcee for his hand, and the emcee backs away, miming horror. The audience laughs, but they're puzzled. It is not entirely clear to them that Ted is a man—maybe the emcee pulled his hand away because she's such a femme fatale?—but it is obvious that this is someone who has violated the Talent Night rules of homespun and shyly showcased minor talents. Ted's is a minor talent, but his production values, from wig to beauty mark, are high—too high for this crowd. Ted flirts with the emcee during the show, but the emcee is stone-faced. I cannot tell, from beginning to end, whether the hostility in the air is a response to Ted's semiprofessionalism, his artifice, or his maleness, but there is something ugly, as there is in the lounge later that night when Merrie sings "My Way" in a pleasant tenor. It is not abusive and not challenging, but there is a coolness, an unwillingness to engage with him as he is.

The show is over. Lori and I talk, looking out at the ocean. She says, "Most crossdressers, they dress in safe places which are just big closets. I think most crossdressers are comfortable as long as it's a safe environment, where they can be seen but not in danger. Although a lot of them need some danger, some milestones—my first time at the mall, my first time in a restaurant."

The evening after the talent show, Felicity comes to dinner en drab, looking like what he is, a heavyset Baptist minister who worked construction in his youth. The headwaiter approaches the table bearing a bouquet of roses. Every night he has become more and more camp and foolishly flattering; the crossdressers are big tippers, moderate drinkers, considerate of the staff, and extremely polite. I don't doubt that they are desirable customers. With a flourish, the headwaiter delivers the roses to Felicity's wife, to applause from our four tables. Felicity puts his big hand on hers and squeezes it. He makes a toast to their thirty years and her goodness and support. He begins to choke up; her remote look never changes. It does not please her that he decided to dress like a man for her tonight. It does not please her that he is so grateful to her for trying to believe that he crossdresses only because he cannot express his warm and nurturing self while wearing trousers. It does not please her, God knows, to sit with a bunch of men in makeup and dresses, some modest, some outrageous, some passable, most not, and call it an anniversary party. It just about kills her that this should be their life, and although she absolutely believes that Jesus will guide them, Felicity's cross-dressing is a cross to bear.

Later they come to talk to me, and when Felicity says that his path may be to minister to the transgendered, his wife puts her hand over her mouth and says, quietly, "Jesus will show us the way." And means, unmistakably, that the way will surely not be this one, that Jesus cannot want her to be the wife of a crossdresser who ministers to the transgendered. Felicity says, "It's like there are three of me in this little boat: the husband, the crossdresser, and the minister. I can hear the falls approaching, and I know, I know with all my heart, one of us will not survive this ride." He begins to cry, and I get tears in my eyes. As I hand him a Kleenex, his wife glares at me and says, "You sure do get involved with your interviews." She must think that it takes some fancy footwork to feel so sorry for the crossdresser and not for his wife, and when I look at her sympathetically, she almost spits. Pity from people like me is not what she wants either. For the remainder of the trip, Felicity seeks me out and his wife avoids me.

I do better with the wives, overall, at Fall Harvest 2000 in St. Louis, Missouri. We all arrive in the last days—not the glory days, if there ever were any, but the last, sad days—of the Henry VIII Conference Center on the frayed edge of the St. Louis airport. In two weeks this place, with its tired decor and dangling fixtures, will be razed to make a new runway. The Henry VIII has bits and pieces of Merrie Old England and bigger bits of St. Louis Generic, circa 1973. It is like a Mel Brooks set with a Spike Lee twist: doorknobs sliding in and out of splintering doors, splotched carpeting, lopsided lamps, and a sparse, disheartened staff composed of black teenagers, some of whom look too young to work, and Bosnian women who look as weary and wary as the American kids. No one is inclined to do much, and when the crossdressers come in with three and four suitcases, the kids and the women all look over sympathetically but without stirring.

The first people I meet in the cavernous lobby are my host, Marcia Lynn, and his wife, Barb. Marcia Lynn is president of the St. Louis branch of MAGGIE (Mid America Gender Group Information Exchange). Throughout the weekend he and the other regulars among the crossdressers will tell me how bad they feel for the staff, whom they've gotten to know during the five years the St. Louis group has been meeting here. “They love us,” Marci says. “We’re friends, a lot of us are fun people. The staff is crazy about us.” Certainly, the other guests, a swingers’ convention, do not tip as well or express solicitude for the staff.

There’s an unexpected resemblance between some of the crossdressers and the swinger wives, who show up for their morning coffee in heavy makeup, sequinned tube tops, fringed miniskirts, and the occasional pair of fluffy bedroom slippers—which do distinguish them from the crossdressers, who stick to their sneakers by day and killer heels at night. By the end of the weekend, some crossdressing couples and swinging couples are sharing Rob Roys in the lounge, but for the most part, the crossdressers express perfunctory tolerance and real disdain for the swingers, who reciprocate with jovial contempt.

At the registration table there are stacks of meal tickets, pamphlets, and information about MAGGIE, the Fall Harvest’s sponsor and the umbrella organization for chapters in Chicago, Minneapolis, Milwaukee, Iowa, Kansas City, St. Louis, northern Indiana, Omaha, and Wichita. Tours of Grant’s Farm, a wildlife preserve, and of the Anheuser-Busch brewery are scheduled for Friday and Saturday. The professional service people for the crossdresser community are also here: Absolutely Picture Perfect, providing videos and formal portraits; Barb’s Large & Lovely lingerie, sizes 1X–8X; the IFGE Bookstore; Shoe Express, ladies’ shoes in sizes 11–15.

Marci runs all over the hotel, happily bustling, scolding, cajoling; he won’t have a real crisis on his hands—aside from the usual lost room keys, forgotten wigs, vendors who fail to show up—until the night of the beauty pageant, when the papered-over gap between the transsexuals and the cross-dressers opens up. Barb works the registration table with her friend Carol, also the wife of a crossdresser. They look like lots of fortyish women in St. Louis: curly brown hair with a little gray at the temples, pastel-framed glasses, comfortable track suits, a little pink lipstick. They are enormously kind and helpful, and they roll their eyes affectionately at their husbands' self-important busyness and excitement, as wives at husband-centered events often do. And in the great tradition of ladies' auxiliaries, they have become important parts of the community, often providing not the point of the event but the web of it: they are the in-house mothers, and Marci publicly thanks Barb every day.

Two crossdressers lounge near the table, although their body language is so coiled and fraught that it is no more like lounging than tae kwon do. They are both thin to the point of disturbance—the emaciated look is almost as common as the matronly one. Other men solve the waistline problem with the severe corseting one sees only in fetish catalogues, Gaultier shows, and Victorian porn, and the rest of them wear large dresses. These two are in tight cocktail dresses, one black spandex, one electric-blue satin with three tiers of flounces from hip to mid-thigh. Awkward and odd in three-inch silk-strapped sandals at two in the afternoon, they pace next to these cheerful dumpling ladies. They don't look so much like men in drag as like people of indeterminate gender with whom something has gone wrong. And they're not happy to see me, either. Throughout the weekend, I get cold-shouldered by the men who find my presence as neither wife nor support staff burdensome, the ones who make it clear that they have to contend with real women ("g.g.'s" is the common, faintly hostile term: genetic gals) plenty the rest of the year. I'm welcomed by a few guys who are happy with their crossdressing, or happy to talk about it, and I'm asked out by two shy, determined men, an accountant and a firefighter, whose previous relationships foundered on the revelation of the crossdressing and who would like to find a nice woman who will accept it, even embrace it.

During cocktail hour I'm approached by Kris and her husband, Leroy, a middle-aged crossdresser. I learn that they are newly married. When he goes off to get a drink, she suggests in a soft Iowa voice that we talk more, later. Her pile of stiff blond curls is not unlike Leroy's. She finishes her drink and looks at me with the sad, amused gaze of a woman who does not kid herself.

"Well," she says, "I put an ad on the Internet for a man in touch with his feminine side, didn't I? Of course, I had in mind a communicator, a romantic, a listener . . . and apparently Leroy read it a certain way. There are so many things you can't say. Most of the wives are not as open as I am. They don't want to say to themselves, 'You're nothing but a people-pleaser, you've been one all your life.' You see yourself as a failure if you can't accept this. The wives don't tell their husbands, they can't tell him because they don't want to hurt him and they don't want to lose him, so they walk a fine line of the truth or they hang on silently and hope his feelings change. Crossdressing is the ultimate form of worship, that's what the men say, and they say they want to develop all those feminine aspects, but I don't feel worshiped. My femaleness is not something Leroy adores—it's *his* femaleness that this is all about. This gift is supposed to be the integration of the feminine side—more nurturing, more open—and the sharing of feminine things *is* very important to Leroy, but he's said that if he can't pass, he'll quit. So I could make him quit, I guess, by telling him the truth, and yet I can't tell him the truth. He'd feel terrible."

I suggest to Kris that *she* feels pretty terrible already.

"I know. I've been thinking of not coming to these things anymore. When he crossdresses, I just don't have a husband. It's not like Dixie and Rebecca, who just seem themselves all the time. He always acts like her husband, not like a nervous girlfriend."

Dixie and Rebecca are standing across the room, both of them in black lace cocktail dresses, Rebecca's floor-length and very Scarlett O'Hara, his mid-calf and rather 1930s, with a dropped waist. Just in case you didn't see him, at six feet, four inches and about two hundred and thirty pounds, he wears a large black polished straw hat with velvet band and dyed black feathers. Dixie and his very pretty wife seem to be having a hell of a time.

"Hey, little lady." Dixie cocks his finger at me John Wayne–style and beckons me over. He is explaining to several crossdressers that if they're stopped by a state trooper they should not try to impersonate a woman or lie. He should know: he's been stopping cars in Alabama for twenty-five years. He plays both roles for us, the menacing trooper and the wetting-his-pants crossdresser hoping to get out of this without newspaper headlines, a beating, or a divorce. The other men laugh, seeming to appreciate his help, and the wives sneak looks at Rebecca, who is holding his hand and twisting around one of his big arms in the historic manner of Southern belles. They are as happy as any other deeply compatible couple, the kind of couple whose pleasure in each other makes them even more golden to the rest of us. Later on, she sits in his lap in the cocktail lounge, and when a stray businessman asks Dixie if he, Dixie, thinks he's a woman, Dixie growls, "I'm a guy in a dress. Of course I don't think I'm a woman. But how about this, pal, we'll ask your wife and my wife who's happier. The winner buys a round." The man backs off and lifts his glass in Dixie's direction. Dixie laughs and kisses Rebecca—"Well, there you go. I'll buy anyway"—and orders drinks for the bartender, the businessman, and me.

Rebecca says, "You know, Dixie's just a people person." (She uses his femme name and his real name interchangeably, and he seems to care as little as she does.) "He goes to the bakery for a loaf of bread, and when he comes back he's got five new friends and four of them are staying for dinner. That's just the way he is, and I guess the dressing up goes with that. Of course I don't mind. Why should I? It's fun for both of us. It's something different, and I'm glad about that. I don't want to just play bridge—I already had a boring marriage."

Rebecca understands that some wives do mind, and she thinks that's too bad.

"I wouldn't have married him if I minded. It's fun, we buy

some fun clothes, and he's always himself. I mean, just look." Dixie is winking at our smiling waitress and setting up a bridge game for later that night.

When the day of the Miss Fall Harvest Pageant arrives, Jim Bridges is busier than a one-armed paperhanger. He is doing makeover after makeover, on his feet from nine A.M. until eight P.M., when the pageant begins: Contemporary Dress, then Talent, then Evening Wear. As I'm sitting on the bed in Bridges' suite turned beauty parlor, Mimi comes by, in undershirt, jeans, and cowboy boots, as Mike. I met Mimi the first night of the conference. He told me he was not going to be in the pageant because he didn't need to be: Mimi's talent was simply in being. That night Mimi was wearing a sort of Heidi the Vampire Slayer outfit—platinum shag, tight black latex corset, suit with arm cuffs, boots, choke collar—and having a fabulous time, flirting, strutting, glad-handing through the crowd, without the restraint or anxiety I see in lots of the men. But now Mike is wandering in and out of Bridges' suite, his powerful shoulders slumped, a slight potbelly over his jeans, distressed that Jim can't fit him in so that he will look "absolutely spectacular" tonight.

Jim cracks jokes and soothes the anxious, perspiring men. The suite has the whiff of a locker room without any sense of team. Each of these men is on his own journey, and although they are kind to one another most of the time, and encouraging ("You go, girl!" "That wig is really good!"), there is no feeling at all that they are in this together or that it is fun.

Jim says, "I want you all to look fabulous. Maybe someone'll get lucky tonight." There is a round of masculine chuckles, and one man says, "I'm all for that!" I ask, "Who would you all want to get lucky with?" and there is complete silence. Jim lifts one eyebrow but says nothing. These men are his bread and butter now, and if he thinks that some of them have a more ambivalent relationship to their sexuality than they acknowledge, he certainly isn't going to offend them by saying so.

"So," Jim says to the man in the chair, "can I tackle those eyebrows?" The man says, reluctantly, that his wife won't let him pluck. Jim is undaunted. "Well, the wife must have her say. Let's just give you exquisite eyebrows tonight." He smooths the lower halves of the man's thick, straight brows with foundation, sets it with colorless powder, and darkens and arches the upper halves with brown powder. When Jim puts a wig of chestnut waves on the man, he looks different, of course. He also looks radiant. He thanks Jim, tearfully—"I can't tell you what it means to me to see myself like this, God bless you"—and the next man hops into the makeup chair. Mike sighs and kicks one pointed toe against the wall.

I volunteer to do Mike's makeup, although I don't think that I can really master the magic of the Scotch tape strips attached to the concealed headband to raise the eyebrows and lids and recontour everything from the jaw up. "Lucille Ball, Loretta Young," Jim says airily. "They did this all the time before everyone had face-lifts." He knows. He did makeup in Hollywood for thirty years, for Joan Collins, Mick Jagger, and a long list of other divas, and when he kept getting bumped from choice assignments "by little blonds with boob jobs who were shtupping the producer," he turned to an unimaginably grateful, large, and uncomplaining clientele: crossdressers.

Jim quickly does the Scotch tape trick and applies Mike's false eyelashes, which I am afraid to do. Nine men wait impatiently, trying on auburn and honey-blond wigs, restlessly looking through the jewelry and false eyelashes and corsets for sale. All the goods are sized for larger-than-average women, to minimize the "King Kong in heels" effect that Jim has been warning them all about.

Mike now looks like a denuded drag queen from the neck up, and like a man ready to mow the lawn from the neck down. As we walk down the hall to his room, he tells me about his very supportive wife, about his teenage boys, who don't know, about his passion for wine making and vintage motorcycles. The worst thing in his life, he says, was Vietnam; his kids are the best thing, especially now that they're old enough to really talk. For forty-five minutes I lean over him, applying foundation, following his instructions, making my own improvisations. So this is what you have to do to stubble, so this is how you diminish the shelf of bone over the eye. I have tried for a subtle, natural look, and when I step back I see what a mistake I've made. With his edges softened, he looks wan and vulnerable, feminized but now lifeless. I put on more eyeshadow, more lip liner. I apply more blush and work it in carefully, then dust a little shimmering powder over it all. Mike looks in the mirror and laughs. Now he looks like Mimi.

"I'd kiss you if it wouldn't mess my lipstick," he says cheerfully, and disappears into the bathroom to get into his pantyhose, his padded bra, and the fierce corset. His wife, stout, handsome, and tired, comes into the room. We introduce ourselves, and she settles down on the edge of the bed with a self-preserving amusement, holding her purse in her lap. I explain that he's dressing.

"Oh," she says, "well, that'll take a while. He really gets into it." She unpacks her overnight case and looks at me closely.

"I helped with his makeup," I say. "Jim was really busy."

"Oh, yeah, I can imagine. I used to help him with it, but—it just took so much time. I said, 'If this is what you want to do, you better get good at it.' "

Mike comes out, as Mimi, his biceps and deltoids gleaming above and below black latex straps, the muscles contrasting with the now small waist. He grins and strikes a pose. He sees his wife and freezes in the doorway, no longer friendly, blunt Mike, not yet wild party-girl Heidi, but a Heidi-in-waiting, hoping that his wife will give him permission to become.

His wife purses her lips. "That's new, huh?"

"Yeah, but if you don't like it, I brought the other one." He points to a more conservative black sheath hanging on the closet door, with cap sleeves and a modest hemline.

She shrugs, massively. "Wear what you want. You ready to go?"

We all walk out together, and I see his wife hail a couple of friends, other wives from the MAGGIE circuit.

The pageant begins with one of the emcees, an older crossdresser, performing Rusty Warren's "Knockers Up," a song from the era of "blue" records: Redd Foxx, Belle Barth, Pearl Williams. Hard-faced and lithe, the emcee lip-syncs Warren's biggest hit, from fifty years ago, and although there is some applause, no one looks very pleased, and the other emcees, Lor and Mary Akers, cut the song off pretty quickly.

Lor and Mary are the new generation for MAGGIE. Lor is a female-to-male transsexual, and Mary, his wife, has been with him since they were a lesbian couple. They are both short and stocky and tirelessly kind, and they both make it a point to check in with me to see if I have met the people I wish to meet. All weekend I see them thanking people, comforting people, sorting out the usual conference problems. The only other "FTM" at Fall Harvest is self-identified—and self-identified only. A petite Cyndi Lauper look-alike, in an ivory pantsuit and rainbow-dyed hair, she claims to be a shaman, a healer, and formerly a man, in her previous life. After she hands me her business card, Mary Akers catches my eye and shakes her head good-naturedly. Mimi pulls the card out of my hand. "Nuts," he says.

The talent portion of the pageant, like the evening wear, ranges from the excruciating (plump, sweet Lor lip-synching, two-stepping, and giddyapping to a loping, sexy cowboy tune) to the pleasant (a dark, strong-featured black crossdresser belts out a gospel tune, and the mere fact that it is actually sung, not lip-synched, and sung well, brings down the house) to the complicated. The complicated performance is Stella's.

Stella, a transsexual, is a warm, giggling blond with a great figure and a flirtatious head toss. Someone tells me she was a successful professional athlete and had her surgery a year ago. On the good side of thirty, fit and energetic, Stella dances and lip-synchs to "Le Jazz Hot," a dopey number from the movie *Victor/Victoria,* in which the point is, of course, that a beautiful woman is impersonating a man impersonating a woman. Stella cuts to the chase. Her adequate lip-synching is background to the real performance, which is simply her body. She strips down, a bit awkwardly, from a tux to a spangly Folies Bergère outfit that clings to her small perky breasts and her bare round ass. Stella shimmies and loosens her hair, which has been hidden under a fedora. Her sexy, very female body is revealed and shaken and shown to every crossdresser in the room. I think she's not much of a dancer, really—there is a certain stiffness in the hips which is very un-jazz—but Jim Bridges and all the other judges (friends of the community, vendors, and therapists) go wild. Stella bows, looking deeply, deeply pleased with herself.

My pal Jeanette, another crossdresser I met the first evening, is next in the show, and I wish he weren't. In his everyday androgynous wear (bandanna, jeans, clogs, and tight T-shirt) he looks like George Peppard in his late-forties prime. In drag he looks awkward, and I blame his girlfriend, Marianne. Jeanette tells me that Marianne sought him out; bisexual and dominating, she loves having a man to dress up in women's clothing. If she's so happy, I think, why doesn't she dress him right? He's in a strange seventies sort of wig, a rayon jersey Liz Claiborne dress, dark hose, and makeup that distorts his features, although I cannot imagine what kind of makeup would not be wrong. If he were a woman, someone would have said to him by now—he's about fifty—"You have strong features, make the most of them." He should have a Diana Vreeland or Gertrude Stein look, powerful and emphatic, with no attempt to take the edge off, because the edge is the glory of those strong masculine faces. What I think, and what impels me to shut up about makeup and clothing when we talk and he asks for suggestions, is that he makes a very handsome man and a plain, awkward woman. Jeanette, smart, appealing, and sensitive, seems to me to have no place in this show, between Stella and the elderly gentleman in tails and leotard, who shows great legs and does an old-fashioned magic act. Jeanette reads from Dorothy Parker's short stories and poetry, and the audience is puzzled, very much as they would be at Miss USA or Miss World. When they say "talent," they don't mean reading.

It's time for the vote. It seems that almost everyone in the small Mr. Fall Harvest division (featured "for the first time ever" at Fall Harvest 2000, "for our female to male guys") wins for something, but the Miss Fall Harvest contestants occasion much shuffling and adding of points. The final three are selected, and Stella is not among them. There is some rumbling, Jim Bridges stalks over from the judges' table, and after a little back-and-forth Mary Akers announces that there was a mixup and everything has been straightened out. Stella, in her low-cut evening gown, is back in the top three. There is generous applause for the gospel singer, for the old magician, even for Jeanette, and there is loud, fair-minded clapping for Stella, who reacts as if she's won an Emmy after years of merely being nominated. Afterward a number of the men mutter that Stella won for showing that she had the equipment, not for doing anything talented with it.

Finally, music begins, and for a moment the judges and the crossdressers and their wives are standing on the dance floor snapping photos, hugging and kissing, sipping their drinks. Within five minutes, all of the crossdressers are off the floor and back to their tables or pouring out into the lobby for a little air. It's too hot and hard to dance in corsets, padding, three-inch heels, heavy wigs, and beaded evening gowns. Even more than that, dancing would melt the makeup and ruin the illusion. Who would they dance with? In the moment of fantasy, even men who don't desire a man as a sexual partner need a handsome man as a prop, as the necessary and missing accessory; a wife is not at all the perfect complement to a ball gown. Not to mention that most of the men—Presbyterian accountants from Cedar Rapids and Lutheran engineers from Omaha—can't dance and never do, not in suits, and not in dresses. I am out on the dance floor doing the macarena with twelve tired, cheerful wives, all of whom have kicked off their shoes and are getting down, hands on rumps, laughing and drinking, until it is so late that we close the joint.

After the cruise, after follow-up e-mails with Melanie and Peggy and more phone calls with the Fairfaxes, I found that I had more to say than I had thought, and more concerns about saying it. I didn't want to demonize or pathologize any sexual preference or behavior that doesn't hurt anyone. I didn't want to make fun of fetishists. Now that our culture has begun to shift toward the notion that reciprocal, mature love between two people, of the same or opposite sex, is not a disease, I didn't want to consign everyone who isn't just gay or straight to the *DSM* junkpile. I wanted to focus on people like Steve and Sue, happily married for thirty years and not caring that with waning hormones they are now often mistaken for a lesbian couple, or on Tory and Cory with their buoyant puppy love, swapping party dresses and playful kisses. I wanted to see crossdressers as so many of them saw themselves. And I did, as with Dixie and Rebecca, but I also saw many of them very differently.

The men I met were, by and large, decent, kind, intelligent, and willing to talk openly; their wives were the same, many under the additional pressure of having to make the best accommodation they can to a marriage they did not envision and do not prefer. But it does seem to me that a passion for a person, or a capacity to love people, is different from a sexual impulse that is directed toward an object or an act and that is greater than the desire for any person. And although one could argue that all desire focused on an object or even an act is a fetish, I don't think so—any more than I think that gender reassignment surgery (even when it's known as gender confirmation surgery) is no different from a tummy tuck. The greatest difficulty people have with crossdressers, I think, is that crossdressers wear their fetish, and the gleam in their eyes, however muted by time or habit, the unmistakable presence of a lust being satisfied or a desire being fulfilled in that moment, in your presence, even *by* your presence, is unnerving. The mix of the crossdressers' own arousal and anxiety and our responsive anxiety and discomfort is more than most of us can bear. We may not mind foot fetishists, but we may not wish to watch either.

The crossdressers of Tri-Ess insist that crossdressing is not about sexuality, and therefore not about sex. They are right about the first, and we can all stop assuming that any man who wears a dress is gay. But they are not right about the second, and their assertion that crossdressing is their creative expression of both genders is unsettling because it is at such odds with their behavior, their natures, and their marriages. These men are as far from gender warriors and feminists as George W. himself. As one wife said to me, "For twenty years he couldn't help with the dishes because he was watching football. Now he can't help because he's doing his nails. Is that different?" For these men, the woman within is entirely the Maybelline version, not the Mother Teresa version, not the Liv Ullmann version, and not even the Tracey Ullman version. There is no innate grasp of female friendship, of the female insistence on relatedness, of the female tradition of support and accommodation for one's partner and of giving precedence to the relationship overall. If you believe that these characteristics are more common to women than to men, these men do not embody them; if you don't believe it, they would argue with you. If there were that kind of understanding, that kind of empathy and female bonding, rather than accessories and tapes on how to walk in heels, these guys would be unable to ask their wives to go through this crossdressing life with them, and everyone, husbands and wives, knows it. They know that if the women insisted on wearing three-piece suits or baseball uniforms in public, and asked their husbands to accept hairy legs, hairy underarms, and jockstraps as part of their sex life, the husbands would not be rushing off to join spousal support groups while cheerfully spending the family's money on bespoke suits and expensive glue-on facial hair. The marriages would be over.

As with the *Ladies' Home Journal* of the 1950s, or *Cosmopolitan* in the 1970s (and 1980s and 1990s), when I read Tri-Ess's advice to wives, I don't know whether to laugh or cry: it's probably your fault but you can fix it, he really needs you but he may not show it, your love will overcome his problem, and a good man is hard to find. If Dickens's devoted, selfless Nancy were alive today—and Bill Sykes, his sadism aside, is exactly the kind of macho, overcompensating, risk-taking guy one might find crossdressing—she would be in a wives' support group, happy to pick out a lipstick, apologizing if they ran out of Slim-Fast just a week before Fall Harvest.

Is it just delicious irony that makes so many people's eyes sparkle when I tell them about my Christian Republican crossdressers? Is it something less sophisticated, like schadenfreude, or even less civilized, like homophobia? It is gratifying to yank the covers off hypocrites: the fundamentalist Christian congressman with his handsome young pages, the feminist and her abusive boyfriend, the priest and his porn.

The widespread assumption is that these crossdressers are hypocrites: publicly lambasting deviance of all kinds and dressing up in private like Little Bo-peep. There is still plenty of Little Bo-peep (and Courtney Love and Scarlett O'Hara), but the lambasting has died down considerably over the last thirty years. In the past, crossdressers were eager to dissociate themselves from gay men and about as interested in feminism as Ward Cleaver. But now, as with the end of the Soviet Union, the unimaginable has happened and the landscape has changed. All the crossdressers I spoke to expressed their admiration for the gay civil rights movement and their hope that whatever acceptance gay people have managed to engender would somehow envelop crossdressers as well. Gay men and women turn out to be their role models in terms of self-respect and civil rights, even if the crossdressers are well aware that the gay community offers them tolerance, not a warm welcome. And feminism, of the women-are-nicer-people variety, although not a part of the wives' lives, adds an unexpected aspect to the men's self-understanding; in their remarks about the burdens of masculinity and the innate nurturing and graciousness of women, in their attempts to connect with Nature and Spirit, they sound like the softest and most Goddess-worshiping of Second Wave feminists.

Almost everything Tri-Ess has said about its members is true: they are straight and traditional men who love their wives and wear dresses. Just as Tri-Ess says, its Christian, conservative, Republican men have a great deal more in common with other Christian, conservative, Republican men than with anyone else. Their wives are not professional women with their own substantial incomes and career paths, and they are not royalty or Hollywood types who expose their spouses' peculiarities and let the muck cling to their kids. They try to make their marriages work, and if the price of a good provider and a decent man is not much sex and a certain amount of constant pain, it is not an unfamiliar bargain. The wives are not uniformly overweight, motherly, and devoid of self-esteem (as some mediocre research has suggested they are), or at least no more so than any other group of middle-class women married young to traditional and dominant men, devoted to home and family, and lacking in advanced education. Juggling the limited resources of time, money, and pleasure, balancing dominance and fear, self-deception and love, selfishness and generosity, crossdressers and their wives struggle with one big difference—his compulsion—and otherwise, just as they have told me all along, they are just like everyone else.

HERMAPHRODITES WITH ATTITUDE

THE INTERSEXED

Beautiful, the doctor says. Ten fingers, ten toes, and the mother's beautiful blond curls. Baby and parents crying with relief, three weary, joyful travelers. They place the baby on the mother's stomach, clamp the cord, and hand the father a pair of slim scissors to cut it. The parents expect both these things—they've seen it done in the Lamaze video, they've seen it on the Lifetime channel. The OB nurse cleans and swaddles the baby quickly while the aide washes the mother's face and changes the bloody sheet under her for a fresh one. They give the baby the Apgar test, a visual assessment taken minutes after birth—a nice experience in most cases, since a baby will get a gratifyingly high score, 8 or 9 out of 10, just by being his or her healthy baby self. It is a high score in this case too, but the doctor shakes his head, in such a small gesture that the father doesn't even see it. The mother sees it, through the anaesthetic, through the sweat, right past the sight of her beautiful baby held tight in the nurse's arms.

Finally, the baby is in the mother's arms. The doctor is thinking fast and trying to hide it. As Dr. Richard Hurwitz instructs in *Surgical Reconstruction of Ambiguous Genitalia in Female Children,* a 1990 training videotape produced by the American College of Surgeons, "The finding of ambiguous genitalia in the newborn is a medical and social emergency." A hundred years ago, midwives examined babies and assigned gender in doubtful cases, or they brought the babies to priests or doctors and the team consulted and assigned gender, and little was made of it until the occasional married, childless woman went to her doctor for a hernia and discovered she had testes, or the married, childless farmer went to the doctor and discovered he had ovaries. Today many physicians regard "genital anomaly" as a dire matter. "After stillbirth, genital anomaly is the most serious problem with a baby, as it threatens the whole fabric of the personality and life of the person," one doctor wrote in 1992; only slightly worse to be dead than intersexed.

The baby is taken to the nursery. The next day the doctor comes in and sits down, and speaks softly. "Your baby will be fine," he says. The parents brace themselves: a faulty valve, a hole where there should be none, something invisible but terrible. "Somehow your baby's genitals haven't finished developing, so we don't quite know right now what sex it is. We're going to run a couple of tests and we'll know very soon. Don't worry. It may be that some cosmetic surgery is required, but don't worry," the doctor tells the parents, who are already well past worrying. "This will all be okay. We can solve this in just a few days. The sooner, the better." As the doctor leaves, he is already calling a pediatric urologist for a consult, getting a pediatric endocrinologist to come over and take a look, getting a geneticist to come on board, to help assign sex and then do what is medically necessary to have the baby's genitals resemble the standard form of that sex.

This scene occurs about two thousand times a year in hospitals all over America. Far from being an exceptionally rare problem, babies born with "genitals that are pretty confusing to all the adults in the room," as medical historian and ethicist Alice Dreger puts it, are more common than babies born with cystic fibrosis. Or, to think of it differently, there are probably at least as many intersexed people in the United States as there are members of the American College of Surgeons.*

Imagine a baby born with an oddly shaped but functional

* In a 1998 article in *The Hastings Center Report,* Dreger writes, "Most people . . . assume the phenomenon of intersexuality to be exceedingly rare. It is not. But how common is it? The answer depends, of course, on how one defines it. Broadly speaking, intersexuality constitutes a range of anatomical conditions in which an individual's anatomy mixes key masculine anatomy with key feminine anatomy. One quickly runs into a problem, however, when trying to define 'key' or 'essential' feminine and masculine anatomy. In fact, any close study of sexual anatomy results in a loss of faith that there is a simple, 'natural' sex distinction that will not break down. . . . For our purposes, it is simplest to put the question of frequency pragmatically: How often do physicians find themselves unsure which gender to assign at birth? One 1993 gynecology text estimates that 'in approximately 1 in 500 births, the sex is doubtful because of the external genitalia.' I am persuaded by more recent, well-documented literature that estimates the number to be roughly 1 in 1,500 live births." The authors of a peer-reviewed 2000 article in the *American Journal of Human Biology* write, "We surveyed the medical literature from 1955 to the present for studies of the frequency of deviation from the ideal of male or female. We conclude that this frequency may be as high as 2% of live births. The frequency of individuals receiving 'corrective' genital surgery, however, probably runs between one and two per 1,000 live births (0.1 to 0.2%)." The Intersex Society of North America bases its estimate of one in 2,000 (which, given about four million births a year, yields an annual total of two thousand births) on "statistics of how

arm. Would one choose an invasive, traumatizing pediatric surgery that almost inevitably produces scarring and loss of sensation, just to make the arm conform more closely to the standard shape? Yet parents believe there must be tests that will show their baby's true sex, and surgery that will ensure and reinforce their baby's true sex, and parents want it to happen, quickly. A few days, even a few hours, of having Baby X is too long. One cannot raise a nothing; when people say, "What a beautiful baby! Boy or girl?" one cannot say, "We don't know." In a culture that's still getting used to children who are biracial and adults who are bisexual, the idea of a baby who is neither boy nor girl, or both boy and girl, is unbearable. How do you tell the grandparents? How do you deliver the happy news that you have a healthy It?

The parents hold the baby, still beautiful, still raw but shapely, and they peer at what is under the diaper. Let's say that what they see is a tiny—even for a baby—tiny penis, technically, a microphallus, both misshapen and far smaller than the standard (less than about two centimeters when stretched out from the body). The prevailing approach for the last fifty years has been to declare that a baby boy with such a small and inadequate penis is better off as a girl. In the

---

many newborn babies are referred to 'gender identity teams' in major hospitals." By any of these reckonings, intersexuality is significantly more common than cystic fibrosis, which has an incidence of one in 2,300 live births, according to the Cystic Fibrosis Research website, and affects some forty thousand children and adults in the United States. The number of fellows of the American College of Surgeons fluctuates a bit from year to year but is about fifty thousand.

straightforward words of surgeons, "Easier to make a hole than build a pole," and the collective medical wisdom has been that a boy without much of a pole, and even more, a man without much of a pole, is doomed to live ashamed, apart, and alone. In the face of the assumption that suicide is likely and profound depression inevitable, a physician with the best intentions and the support of his peers might well declare the boy a girl, remove the micropenis and the testes, fashion labia and a small vagina, and tell the parents as little as possible so as to spare the entire family further anxiety and troubling questions of gender (parents who don't know that their little girl was born a boy are less likely to wring their hands over persistent play with trucks and a refusal to wear dresses). This approach owes a great deal to John Money, a psychologist and the founding director of the Psychohormonal Research Unit at Johns Hopkins, author of some forty books and four hundred articles, whose once-bright star has been dimmed by the case in which he turned little John into little Joan, and in which "John" insisted, heroically, that he was John all along, and resumed life as a male despite John Money's assertion that gender was all a matter of nurture, not nature.

Or let's say that what the parents see is a baby girl with a larger than standard clitoris (more than one centimeter in length). You might not think that this is a problem of "doubtful sex" or confusing genitals, but in infants the gap between clitoris and penis is only about half a centimeter, so the large clitoris that doctors fear will worry her parents every time they change the diaper, and will alarm or even dissuade her future husband, also requires the surgical solution, as early as possible. The surgeries include "clitoral reduction," and if necessary, some enlargement of the vaginal cavity by metal dilators inserted by the parents daily for six months, beginning two weeks postoperatively. Monthly dilation of the seven- or eight-year-old continues into adolescence to prevent narrowing or closure of the vaginal cavity. (The standard for a "good" vagina is one that can be penetrated adequately.) And then, perhaps, following the early vaginoplasty, further molding of delicate and cosmetically pleasing labia may be required.

"Ambiguous genitals," "doubtful sex," "intersexed babies," "male and female pseudohermaphroditism," "true hermaphroditism"—these phrases sometimes describe the same conditions, sometimes very different conditions. Some conditions require hormonal treatment or surgery or both; some require no treatment at all except counseling and time. Symptoms range from the physical anomaly—an unusual-looking set of genitals—to symptoms that will not become apparent until adolescence, to symptoms that will never be apparent from the outside. Some anomalies are defects in the plumbing; others are simply unusual fixtures.

There is a range of medical conditions that fall under the umbrella term "congenital anomalies of the reproductive and sexual system." Boys may suffer from hypospadias, meaning in mild cases that the urethral opening (the "pee hole"), which is supposed to be at the tip of the penis, is perhaps in the glans, on the underside of the penis, or in more severe cases is open from mid-shaft out to the glans, or is even entirely absent, with urine exiting the bladder from behind the penis. Hypospadias sometimes results in ambiguity as to sexual organs, as does Klinefelter's syndrome, which is quite common, occurring in one in five hundred to one in a thousand male births. Most men inherit a single X chromosome from their mother and a single Y chromosome from their father. Men with Klinefelter's inherit an extra X chromosome from either father or mother, and their testes often produce smaller than average quantities of testosterone, so that they don't virilize (develop facial and body hair, muscles, deep voice, larger penis and testes) as strongly as other boys at puberty. (Many also develop small breasts, one of Nature's variations that is often found in those with no intersex conditions at all.) Despite an absence of sperm in their generally small, firm testes, many men with Klinefelter's are never diagnosed because their genitals are typical in appearance.

In androgen insensitivity syndrome (AIS), the body of an XY individual lacks a receptor that enables it to decode messages from androgens (virilizing hormones). AIS results in people with male chromosomes and obviously female bodies; although they produce male hormones, their cells are not sensitive to those hormones, and their bodies never masculinize. There is also partial androgen insensitivity syndrome (PAIS), which typically results in "ambiguous genitalia." The clitoris is large or, alternatively, the penis is small and hypospadic (two different ways of labeling the same anatomical structure). PAIS seems to be quite common, and has been suggested as the cause of infertility in many men whose genitals are typically male.

Among the most prevalent causes of intersexuality among XX (usually female) people is congenital adrenal hyperplasia (CAH), in which the adrenal gland produces an excess of androgens but feminizing occurs at puberty because the ovaries function normally. When excess androgens are produced in utero (sometimes not because of CAH but because an unborn XX baby's metabolism converts hormonal drugs such as progestin, which was frequently administered to prevent miscarriage in the 1950s and 1960s, into an androgen), the female baby may be born with an enlarged clitoris and fused labia that look very much like a scrotum. Sometimes the genitals look typically female, with barely perceptible variations. Sometimes the babies appear to be healthy boys without testes, and it may be that no one in the delivery room thinks anything is amiss. And less often, the babies' genitals are not just misleading but the hallmark of what has historically been called hermaphroditism: truly ambiguous genitals, both male and female, although not a complete set of either.

Monsters, freaks, prophets, border-crossers, portents of disaster—hermaphrodites have been disturbing people for a long time. Ovid wrote of handsome Hermaphroditos, son of Hermes and Aphrodite, whose beauty so dazzled the nymph Salmacis that she longed—as lovers do—to be joined with him. The gods granted her wish, in their quirky fashion, and two turned into one—one Hermaphrodite, now both man and woman. In another version of the myth, Hermes and Aphrodite's child is so completely a mix of both parents, both male and female, that they cannot agree on its sex, and name it Hermaphroditos. In the first version, love flowers so fully that one body can contain two sexes and two souls—a happy ending. In the second, the gods are so baffled that they can do no more than name their child and move on; we hear no more of poor Hermaphroditos, not of love, nor power, nor family life.

The Hippocratics suggested a continuum of gender, much as many contemporary gender theorists do: masculine male at one end, feminine female at the other, masculine women and feminine men along the road, and hermaphrodites smack dab in the middle. Aristotle held that the hermaphrodite was a kind of incomplete twin in whom the ambiguous genitals signaled that almost enough body had been created for two babies, but not quite. The excess body parts, like a sixth toe or a third nipple, were odd and undesirable but irrelevant to the person's "true" sex, which was determined, Aristotle believed, not by genitalia but by the "heat" of the heart.

The search for the "true" sex of the individual seems to me the model that most contemporary physicians have been following. This search, like the search for "true" love, seems composed of equal parts convention, social mandate, human need, and commitment to a dream, and despite all of our trouble and technology, we not only get it wrong more often than not, we cannot even acknowledge that Nature's answers are much more sophisticated than our questions. As Anne Fausto-Sterling writes so neatly in *Sexing the Body*, "Different countries and different legal and religious systems [in seventeenth- and eighteenth-century Europe] viewed intersexuality in different ways. The Italians seemed relatively nonplussed by the blurring of gender borders, the French rigidly regulated it, while the English, although finding it distasteful, worried more about class transgressions."

By the late nineteenth century, physicians were dividing hermaphrodites into three categories based on the identification of gonadal tissue. Individuals having testicular tissue were defined as "male pseudohermaphrodites," and individuals with ovarian tissue were "female pseudohermaphrodites," regardless of the form of the genitals. Only individuals having both ovarian and testicular tissue were "true hermaphrodites." The result of this typology, which relied on "scientific" tissue analysis, was that fewer "true hermaphrodites" appeared: "A body with two ovaries, no matter how many masculine features it might have, was female. No matter if a pair of testes were nonfunctional and the person possessing them had a vagina and breasts, testes made a body male," Fausto-Sterling says. "Additionally," Dreger writes, "given that biopsies of gonads were not done until the 1910s and that Victorian medical men insisted upon histological proof of ovarian and testicular tissue for claims of 'true hermaphroditism,' the only 'true hermaphrodites' tended to be dead and autopsied hermaphrodites." Whatever the intent of the doctors and scientists, in the 1870s people of truly mixed sex, who had been sufficiently common to merit discussion in every country's medical texts, and in the Talmud and Tosefta as well (couldn't shave, like men; couldn't inherit, like women), began to disappear from the records, and took with them their troubling tendency to blur the social issues of the day.

In modern America, we have done our own disappearing act on hermaphrodites: we have turned a lot of baby boys into baby girls, and a lot of healthy baby girls into traumatized ones. A number of scientists and academics have written about this in the last ten years (most notably, the gifted researcher Dreger, the eminently readable and imaginative Fausto-Sterling, the less readable, provocative Judith Butler, and the psychologist Suzanne Kessler), but the person who has almost single-handedly changed both the dialogue on the subject and the surgical practice itself is Cheryl Chase, businesswoman turned activist. If Al Gore had had Cheryl Chase running his campaign, he'd have moved into the White House in January 2001. In a world of megacorporations, tobacco-sponsored rock concerts, and vast, unsavory alliances, Cheryl Chase, perceived as a "true hermaphrodite," first declared a girl, then a boy, then not much of a boy, then operated upon to make her a more suitable girl by removing her "too large" clitoris (what was too large as a clitoris was, of course, terminally too small as a penis), is a modest, relentless, sleepless army of one.

In 1993, she was just an angry woman, distressed and puzzled by the little she knew of her own traumatic history, and anxious to move past it by offering support to people born intersexed (that is, people who have historically been called, with mystery but not much meaning, "hermaphrodites"). She did outreach and information-sharing and complained to anyone who would listen about the unnecessary and usually damaging surgery routinely visited upon babies born with ambiguous genitals—five babies every day, as a conservative estimate, to state the incidence in another way. She picketed; she fired off press releases from her home in the name of her fledgling group, the Intersex Society of North America (ISNA); she organized support meetings and sent out an indignant and well-informed newsletter (now the *ISNA Newsletter*, formerly and more compellingly called *Hermaphrodites with Attitude*). Cheryl Chase and her lieutenants, volunteers all (no one meets Chase and walks away without volunteering their time or making a donation to the cause—she would hardly speak to me until I agreed to send ten dollars for an ISNA videotape), have changed the terms of discussion about surgery and treatment for intersexed babies. The head of pediatric endocrinology at Oakland Hospital now supports the ISNA point of view, the American Medical Association's *Archives of Pediatrics and Adolescent Medicine* has run articles that mirror ISNA's position, and Chase herself has been invited to give talks at the Albert Einstein College of Medicine in New York City, at Denver Children's Hospital, and at the 2000 meeting of the Lawson Wilkins Pediatric Endocrine Society, as the honored closing speaker.

It may be that if you can tell the right story, at the right moment, even people who don't wish to hear will hear. The story of intersex babies is medically complicated, but ISNA simplified it—much to the disapproval of many respected physicians and to the dismay of John Money, whose narcissism and bad faith in the treatment of John/Joan gave John Colapinto's excellent *As Nature Made Him* a sexually provocative, creative, and suavely frightening villain. Through careful study and the pained honesty of intersexed adults, ISNA has undermined the standard argument of good-hearted people ("Surgery may not be a great solution, but it's the only one we have, and it would be worse to raise those poor children as 'nothings' "), and it has undone the peculiar psychological argument that many pediatricians made (parents would be so upset every time they changed a diaper that they would not be able to love the child, and a child with inadequate genitals, especially a boy, would not be able to survive the scrutiny of other children). As common sense dictates, ISNA supports surgery when a medical condition requires it, and encourages families to consult with endocrinologists, knowledgeable psychotherapists, and, if appropriate, the best surgeons they can find. (As every medical student knows: If it works, keep doing it; if it doesn't work, stop doing it; and never go to a surgeon unless you want surgery.)

"We certainly would like to see people become less genderphobic," says one ISNA newsletter, "but we don't think dumping intersex kids into a gender-phobic world with no gender or a 'third gender' is the way to go." Cheryl Chase says, firmly and repeatedly, that physicians who resist reform and feminist theorists who are tantalized by the idea of a "nongender" may have opposite agendas regarding the fabric of our society and its rigid distinctions between men and women, but that both approaches make pawns of the intersexed.

Chase and her small band refuse to be used by any other movement, while making strategic partnerships with NOW and GenderPAC (which had its first national conference in 2001, spreading an umbrella from NOW to the gay Boy Scout and the man fired from Winn-Dixie for crossdressing in his free time). It is ISNA's goal to build a movement without a cult of personality, and it is true that it is not Chase's charm that rouses people. It is the bareness of the truth and her emotionally charged, carefully contained delivery. John Money has charm. Cheryl Chase has changed a small part of how some people live their lives. "Small," of course, only if it doesn't affect you—and it affects more people than you think.

Virilization affected Angela Moreno Lippert when she was twelve years old, living in a small town in Illinois, dearly loved by her parents and grandparents, more than a little popular in elementary school, an A student and a dancer of the kind that fill Miss Beth's School of Movement and Miss Toni-Lynn's Tap and Toe. Angela came home from dance class one day, sweaty and cheerful, flung her clothes onto her bed, and ran a bath. Her mother was on the phone, chatting to a neighbor, keeping half an eye on Angela as she dropped her towel and sank into the tub. By the time Angela stood up to dry off, her mother was hovering in the doorway. Mrs. Lippert took a long, close look at Angela and hung up on her neighbor. She asked Angela to lie down on the couch, and she pulled the towel aside. There, peeking out from between Angela's labia, was her prominent two-inch clitoris, something that Angela herself had noticed over the course of the last year and had considered a source of deep pleasure, although probably worth concealing in the locker room. Angela knew enough to wear double layers of underpants if she was someplace where she might be observed, but she had enjoyed masturbating, without too much guilt, and had assumed that her clitoris was a minor anomaly, like red hair or being double-jointed, except that its location suggested that discretion was advisable.

Mrs. Lippert burst into action. The elderly pediatrician was called, and for the first time in all of Angela's childhood visits, she asked Angela to remain undressed while she brought in a colleague. Both physicians inspected Angela's genitals, but neither of them said anything to her. The Lipperts got an immediate referral to one of the two pediatric endocrinologists in their region. The new doctor was fascinated not only by Angela's oversized clitoris but by the Lipperts' ethnicity. A dozen times she asked if they were sure they weren't from the Dominican Republic, and each time, Mrs. Lippert assured the doctor that the Hispanic side of her family was Mexican, for several generations. (As Angela learned years later, 5-alpha-reductase deficiency, in which apparently female children masculinize during puberty, is exceptionally common in the Dominican Republic.) Evidently concluding that there was nothing more to be learned about the family background, the doctor arranged blood tests and a sonogram. No uterus was found in the sonogram. Angela was told to sit on a hall bench "for what seemed like forever, and when the doctor called me back to the room, it was obvious my parents had been crying." When they left the hospital, her mother gave her a card that Angela still has. It said: "Our dearest Angela, Nothing has changed, you're still our dear sweet little girl, Love, Mom and Dad."

Despite—or because of—the reassurance, Angela became increasingly puzzled and frightened. Why *wouldn't* they still love her? Why *wouldn't* she still be their "dear sweet little girl"? A week later, Angela was admitted to the endocrinology service at Children's Memorial Hospital in Chicago. Her ovaries had not developed properly, the doctors said, and if they weren't removed immediately, they would probably become cancerous: there was great urgency. Angela awoke from the surgery and "felt the packing, like a blanket of wet blood where my who-knew-what-it-was-called had been."

Angela and her parents tried hard to forget the surgery. Angela tried hard to believe that her "growth," as she had come to think of it, had been removed to protect her from cancer, and she clung to that belief until she was about twenty-four. She'd gone into therapy for an eating disorder—a problem that people understood, a problem her mother could worry about openly—and her therapist encouraged her to write for her medical records. She did, and after three weeks during which she feared that the records had been sealed or lost, or that the hospital simply would not release them, they came: twelve pages, of which all Angela could grasp at first was that her pelvic type was consistent with that of an adolescent male. After her gynecologist helped her to decipher the medical terminology, Angela concluded that she probably has

PAIS. The records showed that the "ovaries" the doctors had excised were actually undescended testes, which do pose a significant risk of cancer if not removed. But while they were at it, the doctors extended their sense of urgency to her disturbingly long clitoris, and removed it too, for reasons having nothing to do with the potential for cancer. "I guess they assumed everyone was as horrified by my outsized clit as they were," she says.

Angela went home to Peoria for Christmas and didn't say a word. Months later, a friend sent her Cheryl Chase's newsletter, and Angela regarded the word "hermaphrodite" in a new light. "It hadn't ever been a special word to me. It all sounded nuts, and then I read it and then I saw: this was my experience." She wrote to Cheryl Chase, who wrote back as she always did and always does; they corresponded and they met. Chase convinced her that together they could help intersexed children and prevent the surgical tragedies that most laypeople, and most doctors, considered not merely the lesser of two evils but a pretty good solution. Chase's fervor offered the irresistible choice of health rather than illness, of action rather than regret, and in 1996 Angela Moreno Lippert became an activist for ISNA. She now works with physicians as executive assistant to the director of Surgery and Allied Services at the hospital where she was first diagnosed.

Hale Hawbecker is a regular, middle-of-the-road, white-bread guy with a kind face and a quiet wardrobe. He has a wife and kids and a job as an attorney with the Environmental Protection Agency, and as he says himself, if you'd told him a few years ago that he would find himself sitting in large rooms discussing his genitals with strangers, he'd have called you crazy. But now he sits on ISNA panels, helping the world understand that surgery is not always—not even most often—the best solution to all of the syndromes that tend to produce variant or ambiguous genitals.

"If not for the two essential Hawbecker characteristics, denial and procrastination," he tells a large audience in one of his occasional public speaking engagements, "I would be sitting here a very, very, very angry lesbian. The doctors told my parents I had a very, very small penis. My parents said, 'Do we have to do anything about it now?' And when the doctors hesitated, my parents took me home and wouldn't bring me back." The doctors told the Hawbeckers that their son was deformed and, if not treated surgically, would probably kill himself from shame when he entered adulthood. "I didn't," he says. For a moment, he is visibly uncomfortable, and saddened both by what might have happened and by the actual difficulties of his physical condition. "You could look at my genitals and find them pathetic, or"—and he smiles—"you can look at them as my wife and I do and find them . . . adorable. But they are mine, they are intact, and I will be grateful for the rest of my life to my parents for their decision to let me be."

The audience, some politically minded, some medically minded, and some just curious, exhales in relief. They are horrified by the idea that this perfectly nice, perfectly ordinary man might have been mutilated and forced to live as a girl because his penis was so small as to disturb his doctor.

Hale Hawbecker might never have spoken out if Cheryl Chase hadn't persuaded him to tell his story for the sake of babies less lucky. All roads, all conversations, all the best writings on the intersexed (Dreger, Fausto-Sterling, Kessler), lead to Cheryl Chase, and so does almost everyone else who deals with the subject, in sexology of all kinds, in pediatric endocrinology, in the practical business of civil rights, and in the even more practical business of medical care. Mickey Diamond, the psychologist who helped topple John Money through dogged intellectual persistence, impeccable research, and his own unshakable conviction that he was right and Money was wrong, even when no one else was publicly on Diamond's side, says of Chase, "Well, she has her own agenda, but everything ISNA suggests as the right way to treat these children is the right way. Nature loves variety. Unfortunately, society hates it."

I meet Chase last, after the other folks from ISNA, after pediatricians and surgeons and endocrinologists and historians, after interviewing people who were suicidal from age eleven until the day they discovered ISNA, and people who never thought there was anything wrong with their unusual genitalia and still don't, and people who believe they are a third gender. ("Well, what else am I? What else would you call it?" asked Eugene Pennington, an ISNA member engaged in a lawsuit against the company that fired him. "I have breasts and a penis and I definitely feel some kind of monthly cycle. I live as an effeminate straight man. I don't feel like an unusual guy, I feel like something else entirely. What I really am is a third gender—which no one wants to hear about.")

Chase and her partner, Robin Mathias, a health care data analyst and now also an ISNA volunteer, rent a gingerbread house in a middle-class neighborhood in Petaluma, California. A lush and entangled garden hides the door. Once through the gate and the front porch, I enter ISNA in its two-room entirety. Like any successful nonprofit, it is humming with computers and faxes and graduate student interns, but even the best endowed of nonprofits can't touch ISNA's computer wizardry. It's not the budget or the size of its staff that makes ISNA huge; the truth shall set you free, and the Web shall get the truth out there. Virtual ISNA is huge and deep, an exquisitely organized website with links to everything intersex. Medical professionals, support groups, intersexed people, the parents of intersexed newborns, academics, the wannabe intersexed, and the intersexed-chasers all flock to the site. Those who think they are intersexed, or hope they are intersexed but have no physical sign of intersexuality ("I have terrible PMS. Am I intersexed?" "I can't stand most men, even though I'm a man. Am I intersexed?"), are sent elsewhere, briskly. Those who desire romance with the intersexed are ignored.

ISNA now has money—not a lot, about a hundred thousand dollars, but a geometric leap from the change in Chase's pocket when she started this movement. Doctors, especially pediatricians, send in their contributions, and Chase and her CFO both now receive modest salaries. Before she started ISNA, Chase founded a software development company. She was successful in America and Japan, and there is very little about computers and communication and the art of translation that she doesn't understand. And when, despite all the success, she felt herself falling apart, she volunteered at Tokyo English Life Line (TELL), a crisis hotline for English-speaking people of all nationalities. Suddenly she recognized depression, recognized identity confusion, recognized people in denial, and she began to remember and to wonder. She remembered multiple X rays and blood tests and manual examinations of her vagina and rectum, at the age of seven, and the surgery to trim the testicular part of her ovotestes away. She remembered and she researched and she became a one-woman campaign, not to stop surgery (that would be an understandable goal, given her experience, but it is not her goal, because she is not only a thoughtful person but a logical one), but to stop the shame and prejudice that lead to unnecessary surgery.

In her photographs, Cheryl Chase has bright brick-red hair and the look of a feisty, troubling imp. In person, she is a handsome woman with the concise, controlled movements of a skilled equestrian, which she is. She has the air of an exhausted traveler who knows she's only halfway down the road. Her parrot, Zelda, perches on her shoulder as Robin, wiry, slight, a little skeptical, comes in and out of the room, checking in about a study published in the *Lancet* supporting ISNA's recommendations for the treatment of intersexed infants, checking in about the computers, just checking in. Robin Mathias lives with a woman on a mission, a woman who uses everything around her for the cause, selling me that videotape over the phone, and now three T-shirts before our interview begins, pitching hard for donations in the first issue of the first newsletter ("Send MONEY! No, silly, not Dr. Money—send us cash!"), appearing with Robin in an educational videotape to talk about sexual dysfunction following "corrective" surgery, which means talking about their relationship. Cheryl works all the angles, all the time; Robin watches over Cheryl.

"Parrots, with few exceptions, have no externally discernible sex differences," Chase says. "If you care what sex your parrot is, traditionally you get a laparoscopy done and the surgeon looks at the gonads. I bought Zelda from a breeder, and she had already been laparoscopically sexed and sold as a male. But when I got her, I thought I would prefer her to be a girl and I did a social reassignment on her. No surgical reinforcement."

I look at Zelda, who seems unbothered, and at Cheryl, whose humor is never more pronounced than this small smile.

"It's okay. Zelda doesn't care which pronoun I use." Chase shakes her head. "You know, it's as if there never was and never is common bad medical practice. No doctors treated gay men with electroshock therapy. No one was responsible for Tuskegee. No one sent people with ulcers to psychiatrists."

People with ulcers? What about people with ulcers?

"Ulcers were considered psychosomatic. Remember all

those people drinking milk and going for counseling to calm down? It turns out many of the people with ulcers have a bacterium in their pyloric valve that eats a hole in their stomach. Standard wisdom was that no living thing could exist in such an acid environment. [Paul Thagard's book] *How Scientists Explain Disease* is all about the man who discovered this, who couldn't get heard at medical conferences, couldn't get published. Thinking didn't change at the center, with well-respected pillars of the medical community; it changed, as this changes, on the margins, with people willing to contradict standard wisdom and conventional practice. The journals resist, the doctors resist." Chase leans back; she appears most distant, even indifferent, when she cares the most.

"These were not bad doctors," she says evenly. "A lot of people who feel harmed by this treatment [surgery for ambiguous genitals] will tell you that they were seen by the cream of the crop, by experts. And that's something even doctors don't understand. First they said, 'We don't have to listen to these people, they're crazy.' Then they said, 'It happened a long time ago, and now we do it better, we do it right.' Then they said, 'These people were treated by a handful of bad doctors, and people who have good doctors have good outcomes.' At some point, you have to look for the simple explanation. It's a bad medical model and it causes bad outcomes."

As for ISNA's position, "It's not complicated. We don't say: Celebrate that your kid has severe hypospadias or CAH. We say: No unnecessary surgery, no cosmetic surgery without consent. And more than that, we say: No lying, no shame. We say help the parents and the patients and help them by telling the truth. No lying."

"No lying," Philip Gruppuso says. "No delusions of grandeur on the part of the doctor."

Gruppuso is both a doctor and a dad. He's a bearded, fatherly middle-aged man with twin daughters, now twenty-one years old. When sexual orientation comes up over drinks or at conferences, he tells his colleagues that he wouldn't care if either or both of his girls were lesbians. The straight men around him eye him dubiously, and he's not sure whether they're wondering why he's saying something that couldn't possibly be true, or whether they're wondering if it *is* true—which makes them wonder what kind of normal middle-aged physician and family man from the Bronx would feel that way.

"Physicians, like everyone else, find it hard to change. Not just because of habit but because, in the history of treating these kids, there is an element of homophobia. It doesn't make my colleagues happy when I say this. If you look back at the standard texts of the fifties and sixties, the underlying concern was that people who were 'really' male but looked female would want to have sex with males, and the same for females who appeared male. Homosexual sex was the underlying fear. Not worrying about sexual orientation allows me to think about what's best for the patient and what's good medical practice."

If this criticism has not endeared Gruppuso to his pediatric colleagues, neither has his straightforward assessment of the most common treatment for intersexed babies, and of why it's still more common than what ISNA recommends: "This isn't complicated, it's simple. There are a million ways to screw this up, and most of them have to do with doctors being too sure of themselves, imagining that they control the outcome for sexual orientation and gender identity, and then doing irreversible surgery."

Ten years ago, Phil Gruppuso, now director of research in pediatrics at Rhode Island Hospital and professor of pediatrics and biochemistry at Brown University, was a doctor just like that.

"I was a pediatric endocrinologist and very much in the mainstream. Anne Fausto-Sterling was a colleague and became a friend. I started thinking: I'm a scientist, look at the evidence, look at the follow-ups. I looked at the evidence, and the evidence that this genital surgery is a good idea is just—junk. There's no such evidence that doing surgery on infant genitals for appearance' sake, surgery without consent and which frequently results in sexual dysfunction—there's no evidence at all that this is a good thing. And I am unwilling to harm patients to protect the reputations of physicians who are fine academicians and thoughtful men, but who were—mistaken."

And his advice to doctors confronting their first intersexed baby? "Get a specialist and don't do anything irreversible. Be willing to say, 'It may take a month for us to have a diagnosis and a determination of gender.' Help the parents, help the grandparents, and always, always—it's the first thing we learn as doctors—do no harm. This surgery, and intersexed babies treated by people who don't know what they're doing, does harm."

At the other end of the debate on the treatment of the intersexed are Drs. Richard Hurwitz and Harry Applebaum, creators of the American College of Surgeons training videotape on ambiguous genitals in female children. The tape begins with Vivaldi and a statement of goals: reduce the size of the clitoris, exteriorize the vagina (making it penetrable), and make the genitals cosmetically normal. There is no mention at all of either function or feeling. Hurwitz looks into the camera and says, with quiet confidence, "The treatment of the clitoris depends on its size and the preference of the surgeon." I'm sure it is so; I'm surprised that he says it. "If the clitoris is very large, however," Hurwitz continues as the camera carefully follows the scalpel and the removal of erectile tissue from the clitoris until it folds back into itself, accordionlike, "it may need to be taken care of for social reasons."

It is hard to imagine what social reasons a baby girl might have. It's harder still to imagine how the odd results, described repeatedly in the videotape as cosmetically pleasing, could be anything other than a source of shame and discomfort. Not only are the results not cosmetically pleasing, they're not even good. The surgically altered vaginas and reduced clitorises are painful to contemplate (and even more painfully, the vaginas will probably close and require dilation in the course of the patients' childhood). And according to U.K. research reported in the *Lancet,* follow-up studies of intersexed children show more sexual and psychological dysfunction among those who have had these pull-through vaginoplasties and clitoral reductions than among those who have had no surgery at all. To watch the surgery is to wonder who in their right mind could think that stripping away and excising nerves protects sexual function or that this surgery is not only preferable but essential and urgent—far more so than helping parents help their child to live with a large clitoris, or with a tiny penis, or even with other, more puzzling anomalies.

Not monsters, nor marvels, nor battering rams for gender theory, people born intersexed have given the rest of the world an opportunity to think more about the odd significance we give to gender, about the elusive nature of truth, about the understandable, sometimes dangerous human yearning for simplicity—and we might, in return, offer them medical care only when they need it, and a little common sense and civilized embrace when they don't.

Primum non nocere

AFTERWORD

ON NATURE

People who reveal, or announce, that their gender is variegated, rather than monochromatic or plainly colored in the current custom, have always presented difficulties. Not only is our society distressed by masculine women, feminine men, and the androgynous; even the big man who embroiders, or the wife and mother of three who has a black belt in tae kwon do, a buzz cut, and no makeup in her gym bag, stirs a frisson of discomfort. Gender theorists love the gender-nonconforming as examples of all sorts of things, fundamentalists fear and despise them, and whether they avoid our gaze or deliberately seek to disturb, they are the handy punch line for every fading sitcom.

I sometimes think that our culture is like the Church in the days of Galileo. We will not see, and we will silence and mock, even banish and punish, those who say that what is, is. In one well-designed study, only a third of all "normal" women (for the purposes of this particular study, that would be heterosexual women physically and mentally healthy by self-report and clinical observers' reports) achieved a rating of "classically" feminine. This study described how people actually are—not what they wish to be, not what they imagine themselves to be, but simply how they are—and the results make clear that few of us are what we have nonetheless agreed to believe our gender is. Our cultural standard of gender doesn't resemble gender as normal people experience it. The knife of normalcy cuts sharp and crazy in our culture, and like most trends and fancies, the craziness is only apparent in retrospect. Today we are appalled or amused by medieval or colonial or Victorian nonsense: surgeries for the sexually healthy woman, to make her less so; boarding school sodomy to make little boys into leaders of men; women forbidden to vote or wear pants or practice law; white men forbidden fear and tears; and black people forbidden most everything. I expect my grandchildren will look back on our ideas about gender and sexuality with much the same disbelief.

It's hard to dislodge cultural norms and myths when they provide such reassuring bulwarks in the face of such deep anxiety: the vote will make women barren, the sun moves around the earth. People did not conclude that the sun moves around the earth because they were stupid or narrow-minded; they believed it because it seemed reasonable in light of everything they had heard, or even seen, thus far; then it no longer seemed so evident, and by the time people faced that it was not so, the belief itself had come to seem necessary.

A great many people, sick of news from the margins, worn out by the sand shifting beneath their assumptions, like to imagine Nature as a sweet, simple voice: tulips in spring, Vermont's leaves falling in autumn. There are, of course, occasional mistakes—a leaf that doesn't fall, a clubfoot; our mistake is in thinking that the wide range of humanity represents aberration when in fact it represents just what it is: range. Nature is not two little notes on a child's flute; Nature is more like Aretha Franklin: vast, magnificent, capricious—occasionally hilarious—and infinitely varied. The platypus is not a mistake. The sex-changing animals, coral reef fish and Chinook salmon among them, are not mistakes. The cactus and the blue potato are not mistakes. These plants and animals may not be as reassuring a sight as tulips are, but that doesn't make them deformities.

The hot winters of Australia are not errors. They are just not the cold winters of northern Europe, which typify what winter is, or what it should be, for many Westerners. Surfing at Christmas is not a mistake, not "unnatural," and certainly not proof of the immutable and fundamental superiority of the white Christmas.

After several centuries of confusion, preceded by some early centuries of clarity (at least for Greek gentlemen), we seem to have gotten the difference between gender and sexuality reasonably clear: men are not defined primarily as creatures who only desire women, and sexual desire for men is not the thing that makes a person female. But in our post-Freudian, even post-Lacanian sophistication, in which we wink at the spinsters' "Boston marriage," sure that it must have been a sexual relationship, however unacknowledged, and chuckle knowingly at the "man's man," aware that he is often just that, we seem baffled by the difference between sexuality and temperament, between one's sexual nature and one's personality. There is a whole history of fops and cowgirls, dandies with marcelled waves and tough, wisecracking broads, and where we once understood that one might be male, effeminate, and heterosexual (most of Spencer Tracy's screen rivals for Katharine Hepburn come to mind), or female, masculine, and heterosexual (Rosalind Russell and Thelma Ritter), we seem to have now forgotten. The high-heeled, Chanel-clad lesbian and the football-playing, beer-swigging gay man perplex us, as if surely some norm is violated when a woman who doesn't have sex with men likes lacy lingerie anyway, and a man who doesn't sleep with women enjoys televised sports, cars, and sweatpants. In our collective cultural wish not to be out of it or old-fashioned, we've chosen to be simpleminded. We pretend that sexual orientation and personal style are one and the same and that those who suggest otherwise are trying to make fools of us or hide their shameful preference. Presented with Nature's bouquet of possibilities, a wild assortment of gender and erotic preference and a vast array of personalities, we throw it to the ground.

No one knows why the loss of the mother early in life leads some men to have extramarital affairs and others to cross-dress. No one knows whether transsexuality is a biological result or a mix of the biological, the psychological, and the cultural. (To me, these things seem difficult to unravel—as we are all born into a culture of one kind or another, I'm never quite clear how we strain culture out of our assessments.) No one knows how well most transsexual people do ten or fifteen years after surgery, and no one knows how many transgendered people live happily, and syntonically, at ease with their gender and their sexuality, without ever going near a surgeon, an endocrinologist, or a psychiatrist.

The men and women who devote themselves to these and other questions, to the ins and outs of our private selves, our visions of self, our presentations of self, our hidden histories and baffling communiqués, are psychiatrists, psychologists, sexologists, and academics; they are joined on the field by political activists, surgeons, endocrinologists, entrepreneurs, and lawyers. I am indebted to all of these people, and I, like they, have been taught by the thousands of men and women who live their lives, tranquilly or in distress, with confidence or with trepidation, as cactus and platypus, bearded lady and girlyboy, and push all the rest of us to see that Nature contains multitudes. Although she makes mistakes, these black tulips, these examples of Nature's range, human creativity, and gender's mutability, are not necessarily among them.

BIBLIOGRAPHY

Allen, Mariette Pathy. *Transformations: Crossdressers and Those Who Love Them.* New York: E. P. Dutton, 1989.

Angier, Natalie. "New Debate Over Surgery on Genitals." *New York Times,* 13 May 1997.

Bayer, Ronald. *Homosexuality and American Psychiatry: The Politics of Diagnosis.* Princeton: Princeton University Press, 1987.

Blackless, Melanie, Anthony Charuvastra, Amanda Derryck, Anne Fausto-Sterling, Karl Lauzanne, and Ellen Lee. "How Sexually Dimorphic Are We? Review and Synthesis." *American Journal of Human Biology* 12, no. 2 (2000): 151–66

Bornstein, Kate. *Gender Outlaw: Men, Women, and the Rest of Us.* New York: Routledge, 1993.

Braren, Victor, John J. Warner, Ian M. Burr, Alfred Slonim, James A. O'Neill, Jr., and Robert K. Rhamy. "True Hermaphroditism: A Rational Approach to Diagnosis and Treatment." *Urology* 15 (June 1980): 569–74.

Bullough, Vernon. *Sexual Variance in Society and History.* New York: John Wiley and Sons, 1976.

Chase, Cheryl. "Affronting Reason." In *Looking Queer: Body Image and Identity in Lesbian, Bisexual, Gay and Transgender Communities,* edited by D. Atkins. Binghamton, N.Y.: Harrington Park Press, 1998.

———. " 'Corrective Surgery' Unnecessary: Reply to 'Is It a Boy or a Girl?'" *Johns Hopkins Magazine* 46, no. 1 (February 1994): 6–7.

Colapinto, John. *As Nature Made Him: The Boy Who Was Raised as a Girl.* New York: HarperCollins, 2000.

DeJong, Tom P.V.M., and Thomas M. L. Boemers. "Neonatal Management of Female Intersex by Clitorovaginoplasty." *The Journal of Urology* 154 (August 1995): 830–32.

Devor, Holly. "Female Gender Dysphoria in Context: Social Problems or Personal Problems." *Annual Review of Sex Research* 7 (1996): 44–89.

———. *FTM: Female to Male Transsexuals in Society.* Bloomington: Indiana University Press, 1997.

———. *Gender Blending: Confronting the Limits of Duality.* Bloomington: Indiana University Press, 1989.

Diamond, Milton. "Sexual Identity, Monozygotic Twins Reared in Discordant Sex Roles and BBC Follow-up." *Archives of Sexual Behavior* 11, no. 2 (1982): 181–86.

Dreger, Alice Domurat. "'Ambiguous Sex' or Ambivalent Medicine?" *The Hastings Center Report* 28, no. 3 (May/June 1998): 24–35.

———. *Hermaphrodites and the Medical Invention of Sex.* Cambridge, Mass.: Harvard University Press, 1998.

———. *Intersex in the Age of Ethics.* Hagerstown, Md.: University Publishing Group, 1999.

Fausto-Sterling, Anne. "The Five Sexes: Why Male and Female Are Not Enough." *The Sciences* (March/April 1993): 20–24.

———. *Sexing the Body: Gender Politics and the Construction of Sexuality.* New York: Basic Books, 2000.

Garber, Marjorie. *Vested Interests: Cross-dressing and Cultural Anxiety.* New York: Routledge, 1997.

Glassberg, Kenneth I. "Gender Assignment in Newborn Male

Pseudo Hermaphrodites." *Urologic Clinics of North America* 7 (June 1980): 409–21.

Green, James. "Getting Real About FTM Surgery." *Chrysalis: The Journal of Transgressive Gender Identities* 2, no. 2: 27–32.

Halberstam, Judith. *Female Masculinity.* Durham, N.C.: Duke University Press, 1998.

Hermaphrodites with Attitude/ISNA News. Newsletter of the Intersex Society of North America. Petaluma, Calif.: 1994–.

Kessler, Suzanne. *Lessons from the Intersexed.* New Brunswick, N.J.: Rutgers University Press, 1998.

Mazur, Tom. "Ambiguous Genitalia: Detection and Counseling." *Pediatric Nursing* 9 (November/December 1983): 417–31.

Miller, Rachel. *The Bliss of Becoming One! Integrating "Feminine" Feelings into the Male Psyche, Mainstreaming the Gender Community.* Rainbow Books, 1996.

Money, John. "Psychologic Consideration of Sex Assignment in Intersexuality." *Clinics in Plastic Surgery* 1 (April 1974): 215–22.

———. *Sex Errors of the Body: Dilemmas, Education, Counseling.* Baltimore: Johns Hopkins University Press, 1968. Reprint, 1994.

Morris, Jan. *Conundrum: An Extraordinary Narrative of Transsexualism.* New York: Henry Holt, 1986.

Nanda, Serena. *Neither Man nor Woman: The Hijras of India.* Belmont, Mass.: Wadsworth Press, 1990.

Newton, Esther. *Margaret Mead Made Me Gay.* Durham, N.C.: Duke University Press, 2000.

———. *Mother Camp: Female Impersonators in America.* Chicago: University of Chicago Press, 1972. Reprint, 1979.

Raymond, Janice. *The Transsexual Empire: The Making of the She-Male.* Boston: Beacon Press, 1979.

Rudd, Peggy. *My Husband Wears My Clothes: Crossdressing from the Perspective of a Wife*. Katy, Tex.: PM Publishers, 1999.

———. *Crossdressing with Dignity: The Case for Transcending Gender Lines*. Katy, Tex.: PM Publishers, 1999.

Solomon, Alisa. *Re-Dressing the Canon: Essays on Theatre and Gender.* New York: Routledge, 1997.

Sontag, Susan. "Notes on Camp." *Partisan Review,* Fall 1964: 515–30.

Stoller, Robert J. *Sex and Gender: On the Development of Masculinity and Femininity.* Vol. 1. New York: Science House, 1968.

Sullivan, Louis. *From Female to Male: The Life of Jack Bee Garland*. Boston: Alyson Publications, 1990.

Van Seters, A. P., and A. K. Slob. "Mutually Gratifying Heterosexual Relationship with Micropenis of Husband." *Journal of Sex & Marital Therapy* 14, no. 2 (1988): 98–107.

A NOTE ON THE AUTHOR

Amy Bloom is the author of two collections of stories, *A Blind Man Can See How Much I Love You* and *Come to Me*, and of *Love Invents Us*, a novel. Her work has appeared in *The New Yorker*, *Antaeus*, *Story*, *Mirabella*, *Vogue*, *The Atlantic Monthly*, and *The New York Times Magazine*, among other publications, and in many anthologies here and abroad, including *The Best American Short Stories*; *Prize Stories*: *The O. Henry Awards*; *The Secret Self*: *A Century of Short Stories by Women*; and *The Scribner Anthology of Contemporary Short Fiction*. Also a practicing psychotherapist, she lives in Connecticut and teaches at Yale University.

A NOTE ON THE TYPE

The text of this book is set in Linotype Sabon, named after the type founder, Jacques Sabon. It was designed by Jan Tschichold and jointly developed by Linotype, Monotype and Stempel, in response to a need for a typeface to be available in identical form for mechanical hot metal composition and hand composition using foundry type.

Tschichold based his design for Sabon roman on a fount engraved by Garamond, and Sabon italic on a fount by Granjon. It was first used in 1966 and has proved an enduring modern classic.